# EMERGING FACES
## the Mexican-Americans

K

# EMERGING
# FACES

## the Mexican-Americans

Y. ARTURO CABRERA

San Jose State College

WM. C. BROWN COMPANY PUBLISHERS

72-1723

Copyright ©1971 by Y. Arturo Cabrera

Library of Congress Catalog Card Number: 79—135153

ISBN 0—697—06002—0

Second Printing, 1971


Printed in the United States of America

# contents

# preface

Discussions today about Mexican-Americans most frequently deal with culture conflict and social pathologies. Here and there students working for advanced degrees undertake delimited studies. Trade and governmental publications are infrequent. Views from Mexican-Americans themselves are not heard.

In search for the positives of the Mexican-American, students must be persistent researchers. They find scattered bits of information in historical papers, folklore society reports, journals from the social sciences, and occasional articles in newspapers and popular magazines.

We are in an era of ethnic culture awareness today, and there is a demand for publications about Mexican-Americans. Not much is available. This reflects past failures of educational and social institutions in perceiving conflicts of the group. At the national level negligible resources are invested and directed to this end.

My purpose is to speak on selected issues as a Mexican-American, not necessarily interpreting for all, but expressing a particular orientation and response to events. The status of the Mexican-American group itself is one of many contradictions, and I have attempted to reflect this.

I wish to state clearly that for years distinguished scholars and writers, Spanish-speaking and Anglo-American alike, have expressed a concern. Regrettably, the impact of their studies on the American public has been limited.

Hopefully this publication will stimulate readers to inquire openly about Mexican-Americans.

# acknowledgments

The number of individuals, groups, and communities which in one way or other have influenced this writing is vast. I am profoundly stirred by the frequent examples of commitment, insight, and diversity, and I am indebted to all. The responsibility, however, for viewpoints and interpretations is mine alone. The California State College system is thanked sincerely for the opportunity to undertake this writing.

Words incompletely express my sense of gratitude for the sustained support and encouragement from Jo, my wife, and my sons Arthur and Ronald.

# Introduction

Mexican-Americans are in all stages of acculturation in America. Today they range from the classic description of middle class to the image familiar especially in the 1930s of the rural revolutionary *peón* found in American textbooks. The story of the Spanish-speaking in America starts over 450 years ago. They were on American soil and founded communities before the Pilgrims landed on Plymouth Rock.

In the spring of 1513, twenty-one years after Columbus' first voyage of 1492, Juan Ponce de León landed on the southern coast of Florida. Hernando Cortez arrived in Mexico and founded Vera Cruz in 1519. Juan de Oñate explored north of the Rio Grande in 1598 in the area that is today the American Southwest. Forty years before Jamestown, the Spanish founded St. Augustine, Florida, in 1565.

The persistent search for the "Seven Cities of Cíbola" in the Southwest by Francisco Vásquez de Coronado has provided material for many glowing historical as well as fictional accounts. About one hundred years later, after the first settlements in New Mexico and San Diego, California became a reality, and the saga of the Californianos unfolded.

Other historical dates are important. The Mexican War in 1846–1848, known in Mexico as the North American Invasion, is remembered as the occasion when Mexico in defeat surrendered an immense territory. This was followed by the Gadsden Purchase and more Southwestern states became part of the United States. These are bitter roots in history for Mexican and Mexican-American alike and go far in explaining some of the suspicion held toward the Colossus of the North.[1]

In the dim recesses of the Mexican heritage are the Toltecs and their creative culture which was adopted at least in outward form by the warlike Aztecs and other Nahuas.

1. See Ramón Eduardo Ruiz, ed., *The Mexican War: Was It Manifest Destiny?* (New York: Holt, Rinehart and Winston, Inc., 1963) for views by Mexican writers as well as arguments for and against the justification of this war by Anglo-American authors.

This civilization is highlighted by the archeological marvels of Teotihuacan, Monte Alban, and Mitla, the fabulous city of Tenochtitlán and the Floating Gardens of Xochimilco, as well as heroic feats of the Aztec emperors Moctezuma and Cuautémoc. Archeologists report this Indian civilization superior in ways to that of Europe of the time.

Though Spanish-speaking peoples were already living in the Southwestern sector of the United States at the time the New England and Atlantic colonies were being founded, the number of colonists continued small for a long time. It was not until sixty years or so ago that Spanish-speaking or Mexican people in great numbers came to the United States. Many of these later immigrants came chiefly from the northern and central plateaus of Mexico, seeking relief from intolerable living conditions, the products of frequent revolutions, dictatorial and feudal-type exploitation, and because the American railroad and agricultural interests and mining interests actively recruited them to fill the immediate needs for "unskilled" labor in a booming economy.

This burgeoning tide of Mexican immigrants included many classes of people leaving their homeland for diverse urgencies. Some were revolutionary soldiers fleeing changes in the fortunes of war. Intellectuals, professors, and teachers, finding governing ideologies and action totally inhospitable to them, joined the stream. Rural and urban dwellers alike, finding their roots destroyed, were also included. Politicians in disfavor found they were completely dispensable, and prudence dictated their quick absence from Mexico. And in large numbers indeed were the young and the old, the dependent and the helpless, along with the strong and the able, the men and women who saw no immediate hope for security in a war-torn and devastated country.

These people and others for many individual reasons looked forward to what to them was still very much a part of Mexico historically and culturally. The technical difference was that ownership and control of the land and institutions now lay in the hands of the Anglo-Americans.

Plans for the future were postponed in many cases. It was necessary first to eat and to provide shelter and security for families. Time would permit, it was thought in many cases, the return to Mexico and to the known and familiar cycle of activities. This return was not to take place for many of these brave people. But part of the consequence of this frame of thinking was that many of these immigrants did not at all consider cutting ties and loyalties loose from Mexico. No rationale was generated for accommodating and integrating purposefully into the Anglo culture and society. Consequently, many of these immigrants unquestioningly retained much of their culture, language, and religion quite effortlessly through the insulation of their *colonias* on the one hand and the isolation by the dominant culture on the other.

Out of this long history were born two romanticized stereotyped images. One of them includes dark-eyed *señoritas* with roses in their hair, dark men on spirited horses, excitement at three in the afternoon with the running of the bulls, and sprawling haciendas or ranchos managed by the Hispanic aristocracy in a gracious and courtly style.

The other stereotype reflects a folk culture which evokes images of the *indio* and of the *peón*, both products and victims of a feudal system which was part of the heritage from Europe.[2]

From this past history Mexican-Americans inherit similarities which make them identifiable as a group. The Spanish language is a bond. Language is not only a means of communication between members of a group, but it is a living symbol of a culture which is unique when contrasted to the Anglo-American. It serves to unite.

Religion is another bond. The Spanish *Conquistadores* were accompanied by missionaries who planted the Catholic faith alongside the flag. The Church is generally conceded to be an important solidifying factor for the Mexican ethnic group.

The family is unifying. Usually the Mexican family is larger than the American. It includes parents and children, but also an extended circle of relatives as well. This extension of family permits an individual to feel secure and sufficient within his group. There is less need for involvement in community and civic affairs as a way of satisfying social and personal expression. The amenities of family life draw people together. Respect, courtesy, and affection are shown elder family members.

A man is defined. Internal qualities are valued over external symbols. Great value is placed on personal, spiritual, and ethical qualities. These nurture serenity and minimize the compulsion for conspicuous material success which characterizes the Anglo culture and is best exemplified in goals of financial gain, constant activity, and competitive drive.

The ideologic contrasts between the two cultures' concepts are unmistakable. Mexican-descent people frequently criticize Anglos for being boorish, unfeeling, and greedy. No properly-reared Mexican would ever lose sight of the basic values of life. A person who is *bien educado* (well-reared) always observes the rituals and amenities of good taste. This is a pervasive and cherished interpersonal quality in Mexican behavior and attitude.

Another sharp contrast lies in the matter of time perspective. Mexicans are frequently described as present-time-oriented. Nonsense! Mexicans, rather, have defined values so discriminatingly that priorities are well established. The important matters have a precedence. The good things of life are

---

2. Historians believe the warrior-priest hierarchies of the Mexicans were also examples of feudal lords.

to be savored fully unless overriding reasons require postponement. Certainly those matters which must be attended to today are not put off for tomorrow.

Countless Mexicans and their children have contributed to the growth of America through their labor and talents. Families that rise and are at arduous work by dawn surely are not easy-going by any definition.

Today, many Mexican-Americans are among the disadvantaged who are submerged by discrimination and prejudices, substandard housing, unemployment, inadequate education, and absence of political voice and power. This disadvantage is real in great measure for the total group because prejudiced Anglo-Americans do not distinguish between individuals within the ethnic group. For these Anglos a Mexican is a Mexican. No distinctions are drawn. Because he is different in a number of ways—appearance, language, culture, religion—he automatically, though at times unconsciously, is considered second-class.

Acculturation creates unexpected problems. The most common complaint from the hard-core *barrio* is that acculturated Mexican-Americans lose their Mexicanism. The leadership potential of these individuals is reduced because they lose touch and feeling for their old community, yet these persons are the ones frequently selected by the established power structure as representatives or interpreters of social problems facing Mexican-American groups.

All that has been said so far, then, illustrates the standard story or explanation of the Mexican-American, and much of this is accepted without any question. How much of this is true or how great are the contemporary variants are basic questions for exacting studies.[3] It is necessary that questions be raised regarding many of the present interpretations about Mexican-Americans if sounder insights are to emerge. Today what passes as *understanding* the Mexican-American is at times distorted, polarized, and absurd.

The following chapters are intended to paint in broad strokes a picture of Mexican-Americans.[4] Some views about the group today are credible, but others are subject to grave criticisms and serious questions. Some of these views appear to be examples of nondiscriminating thinking and blanket

3. It is not possible to list all contributors about Mexican-Americans, but any list surveying the last thirty years would surely include these names: Ralph L. Beals, Emory S. Bogardus, John H. Burma, Jose Manuel Espinosa, Ernesto Galarza, Manuel Gamio, Manuel H. Guerra, M. Sylvius Handman, Norman D. Humphrey, Sigard Johansen, Robert C. Jones, Oscar Lewis, Herschel T. Manuel, Julian Samora, George I. Sanchez, Lyle Saunders, Donovan Senter, Paul M. Sheldon, and Paul S. Taylor.
4. Some of the general conditions about Mexican-Americans may also apply to other Spanish-speaking groups. But this writing raises no pretense of sweeping generalizations for or about other Spanish-speaking groups. Rather, the story and the ethos of these other Spanish-speaking peoples will best be served by writers from those ethnic groups and those who may have special insights and competencies.

stereotyping. An immediate and high priority is stressed for the escalation of studies, programs, writings, and involvement of and with Mexican-descent people of the United States. Finally, the meaningful goal in America is integration as a bilingual and bicultural group into a pluralistic society which owes its growth, strength, and achievement to the blood and sweat of many diverse ethnic, racial, and cultural groups.

## BIBLIOGRAPHY

ADAMIC, LOUIS. *A Nation of Nations.* New York: Harper and Brothers, 1945.

BURMA, JOHN H. *Spanish-Speaking Groups in the United States.* Durham, N.C.: Duke University Press, 1954.

CABRERA, Y. ARTURO. "A Study of American and Mexican-American Culture Values and Their Significance to Education." Dissertation, University of Colorado, 1963.

CAMPA, A. L. "Mañana Is Today." In *Southwesterners Write,* edited by T. M. Pearce and A. P. Thomason, pp. 291–304. Albuquerque: The University of New Mexico Press, 1946.

FAIR EMPLOYMENT PRACTICES COMMISSION. *Californians of Spanish Surname.* 455 Golden Gate Avenue, San Francisco, California, May 1954.

KIBBE, PAULINE R. *Latin Americans in Texas.* Albuquerque: The University of New Mexico Press, 1946.

McWILLIAMS, CAREY. *North from Mexico.* New York: J. B. Lippincott Co., 1949.

MADSEN, WILLIAM. *The Mexican-American of South Texas.* New York: Holt, Rinehart and Winston, 1964.

ROBINSON, CECIL. *With the Ears of Strangers: The Mexican in American Literature.* Tucson: The University of Arizona Press, 1963.

RUIZ, RAMÓN EDUARDO, ed. *The Mexican War: Was It Manifest Destiny?* New York: Holt, Rinehart and Winston, Inc., 1963.

SAUNDERS, LYLE. *Cultural Differences and Medical Care.* New York: Russell Sage Foundation, 1954.

SAVETH, EDWARD N. *American Historians and European Immigration, 1875–1925.* New York: Columbia University Press, 1948.

WATSON, JAMES B., and SAMORA, JULIAN. "Subordinate Leadership in a Bicultural Community." *American Sociological Review* 19, August 1954, pp. 413–421.

WOODS, SISTER FRANCES JEROME. *Mexican Ethnic Leadership in San Antonio, Texas.* Washington, D.C.: The Catholic University of America Press, 1949.

chapter **2**

# Treatment in the Literature

Readers unconsciously tend to identify with personalities and themes in the literature used for educational purposes as well as for pleasure reading.[1] If a person sees his intimate group and the culture with which he identifies treated favorably, he feels good about it. He sees his ethnic or social group accepted in the dominant culture and he feels good. He belongs.

Children of Mexican descent have the same need as all other children for positive identification as they identify with personalities and historical events in the required reading. This is a truism. Observers know there is a limited amount of literary and instructional materials available for the positive study of Mexican-Americans. One national association after deliberating the matter of ethnic images in textbooks concluded that

. . . books are the most obvious and the most fundamental requirement for any program seeking to create and expand international understanding, [and] no matter what subject-matter area is under consideration, the teacher can accomplish very little without the necessary tools. Good will and enthusiasm are a *sine qua non*, of course, but they alone are not enough.[2]

As the search for materials grows, it becomes increasingly clear that the role of the Mexican-American is neglected and America is depicted almost exclusively Anglo-Saxon in personality and culture.[3]

Communities, and especially teachers, must understand that textbooks project a set of selected views. Those views of the national culture highlighted are those acceptable to the power structure. It can be said unequivocally that much, if not most, of the printed material in use today in public schools and

1. Radio and television are also important instruments. Recently television has been challenged for the use of demeaning stereotypes in advertising.
2. *Teaching About Other Countries and People in Elementary School*, Department of Elementary School Principals, National Education Association (Washington, D.C.: NEA, 1201 Sixteenth St., N.W.), June 1960.
3. Aaron N. Slotkin, "The Treatment of Minorities in Textbooks," *Strengthening Education*, vol. 16, 1964; *Education Digest*, October 1964, pp. 21–23.

higher education is critically limited in quantity, and it tends to consistently depict Mexican-Americans and their ethnic culture in uncomplimentary stereotyped themes.[4] (Stereotyping of Anglo-Americans also takes place. Latin-Americans frequently think of them as henpecked and common.)

The majority community fails to note the absence or the inaccuracies of the stereotype; so they see no problems. It never occurs to them to ask why no Mexican-Americans appear in the thousands of printed materials used in the schools and in the avalanches of popular reading in the periodicals and newspapers in America.[5]

As pressures build for the initiation of Mexican-American or Chicano Studies, and materials for these new courses are not readily found, panic mounts among school administrators, librarians, and teachers of the courses. Student outbursts may occur as a result of frustrated impatience.

Literature casting Mexican-Americans in positive roles is needed urgently today. Mexican-American as well as Anglo children must have these positive experiences if intergroup conflict is to be reduced and if Mexican-American children are expected to grow normally in self-esteem.

An alarming shortage of materials regarding Mexican-Americans was revealed in a recent survey of elementary and secondary curriculum resources.[6] These are the shortcomings found:

1. There is a serious shortage of educational media at all levels from kindergarten through high school.
2. Groups are mostly presented as a "social problem" or a "security threat" during a specific period.
3. Current contributions are most likely to be ignored.
4. Facts are often distorted, especially in fiction.
5. Youth resent the absence of ethnic representation in illustrations. They equally resent the repainting of existing pictures to simulate mixed representation.
6. There is a shortage of children's books showing the specific problems of all ethnic groups presented in a realistic manner.
7. There is a serious shortage of children's books presenting those problems of minority children that are not concerned with race.
8. The practice of linking the various ethnic groups with stereotyped occupations is unrealistic.
9. There is a need for more material written by qualified members of all ethnic groups.
10. There is a need for professional organizations and publications to include in their reviews materials that have been found to be unacceptable for purchase.

4. Cecil Robinson, *With the Ears of Strangers: The Mexican in American Literature* (Tucson: The University of Arizona Press, 1963).
5. Robert D. Kranyik, "A Comparison of the Images of Mexico Portrayed in Elementary Social Studies Textbooks and Possessed by Connecticut and Mexican Teachers" (Ph.D. dissertation, University of Connecticut, 1965).
6. "Multi-ethnic Materials Survey," Northern Section Human Relations Committee, California Association of School Librarians, January, 1970. This finding is also applicable to the Oriental American and the American Indian.

The conscious and unconscious reaction to images found in the literature read in school or at home becomes critical. When these real or fictional models are presented favorably to the child, they become desirable sources of identity. If these models are devalued or subordinated, and if this happens frequently, they will adversely influence a child's view of himself.

When pervasive negative stereotypes of particular groups exist, individuals from these distinct groups will suffer painful psychological harm. The usual treatment of minorities in our best texts is to select the most picturesque aspects of the group, to place the people in a quaint and exotic culture setting—for example, plenty of burros, cactus, and adobe huts—and to surround them with poverty. This is the common model for the "study" of the Mexican-descent people.[7]

Any identity with these public images can only serve to reduce self-acceptance or to create unnecessary obstacles to the educational or social achievement of a Mexican-American. Where failures are created, they become a loss to the total community as well as to the person and his family. When the ethnic image or cultural characters with which people identify are consistently notorious or unflattering, the cumulative effect reaps its destructive toll in the lives of the minority young as well as in the lives of adults already caught in a web of self-doubt and growing conflict. This situation also does nothing to correct the conscious or unconscious attitude and behavior of the total community toward the minority person or group.

The greatest catastrophe, perhaps because it is so unconscious, is the bias of total omission of groups of people: the Indian, the Negro, the Oriental, the Mexican-American, and other minorities. Literally, they become the people who were not.

A review of twenty-nine selected books found one great fault in the treatment of Mexican-Americans. They were simply not mentioned. It was total omission.[8] What can be more ignominious for a people whose presence and culture are felt throughout the Southwest? To be totally ignored rather than pointedly profaned is like giving the condemned a choice of dying by the gallows or by the firing squad. This omission simply says to a minority youth, "You are a nobody."

Images of virile men, comely women, sterling qualities, and noble deeds are to be expected in the literature and history texts because Mexicans and their people too are these kinds of personalities. Unfortunately, this is not the image children of Mexican descent react to from reading materials in and out of the schools.

7. Mildred Mulkin Smith, "An Analysis of Basal Reader Stories with Cultural Settings Outside the United States" (Ed.D. dissertation, Indiana University, 1959).
8. Gloria T. Blatt, "The Mexican-American in Children's Literature," *Elementary English*, April 19, 1968, pp. 446–451.

What is the usual literary menu about Americans of Mexican descent? Physical environment and climate are rustic and folk societal. The quaint and cute are portrayed, and unfailingly the whole scenario develops like a comic opera. What can be elevating about this constant mishmash for anyone? The captive Mexican-American child is subjected repeatedly to this caricature. If the Chicano is sensitive to the drama, he learns to hate himself. The less perceptive child, too, continues to be saturated with this during his formative years, and he internalizes mixed feelings. Frequently his confrontation with society is later as an adolescent or a young adult, and it is a bitter revolt.

One cannot choose from either alternative, but in either case there is personality disorientation and an ambivalence, if not outright hostility, toward the total community. Neither the process nor product is consistent with the avowed aims of public education in a democratic society.

What factors contribute to this dilemma? Obviously many do, for it is interrelated and complex, but one factor of importance to school people is the printed matter which presents the grist for the educational mill. School personnel need to be sensitive to the portrayal in and out of print of Mexico and Americans of Mexican descent.[9] This portrayal in its deficiency serves further to create feelings of inadequacy and also reinforces prevailing community attitudes which are inimical to Mexican-Americans as a group. The image-reflection found in the reading materials selected especially by school people is therefore crucial. Discredited ideas and attitudes are perpetuated by the indiscriminate use of old texts. These errors gain authority and acceptability among the young by virtue of being in a book.[10] The correction of the history or literature is clearly important for both Anglo-American and Mexican-American children.[11]

According to one source, Mexican-Americans came of bibliographical age in the 1940s. This view notwithstanding, Americans of Mexican descent continue as a neglected minority. The mimeographed reams of opinions about social and educational concerns of Mexican-Americans have not made much of an impact on American institutions and people.

Few books published in the last several decades about multiethnic groups have much pertinence for Anglos or Mexican-Americans. Two thou-

9. Edward N. Saveth, *American Historians and European Immigrants: 1875–1925* (New York: Columbia University Press, 1965).
10. UNESCO, *Bilateral Consultations for the Improvement of History Textbooks*, July 1953 (Nendeln, Liechtenstein: Kraus Reprint, Ltd., 1966).
11. The conclusions of a review of 30 current textbooks were that controversial issues in general were treated in a fair and objective manner and that the content was virtually free of concepts, terms, or phrases that might contribute to prejudice or misunderstanding (Robert Addison Meredith, "The Treatment of United States-Mexican Relations in Secondary United States History Textbooks Published Since 1956" [Ed.D. Dissertation, New York University, 1968]).

sand books have been published annually for children and young people. But until very recently, few, if any, attempts were made in these publications to portray accurately multiracial and multiethnic societies. . . . We do admit that over the years we have failed in writing and disseminating materials which truly advance education for democratic human relations.[12] [Note: In spite of the conference theme, the crisis Mexican-Americans and other Spanish-speaking groups are facing was treated in a most *insignificant* manner.] Fugitive papers, essays, and student reports which constitute the bulk of the available writings contain noticeable deficiencies.[13] The noncommercial quality of the papers limits their circulation. They are frequently superficial in content; they continue to use historical stereotypes; they are based on incomplete information; and they tend to be written by the wrong people.[14] Further, too few writers of Mexican descent either attempt to write or succeed in getting their documents published. Some reasons for failure to publish about Mexican-Americans and by Mexican-Americans are known. Too limited resources are invested in promising studies. Financial support is not available, and technically qualified personnel are not released to concentrate on the task. A commitment to this area of writing is regrettably missing.[15]

Financial resources continue to be withheld largely because Anglo-American institutions and agencies are traditionally indifferent to concerns of Mexican-Americans. This classic example of institutional myopia and disregard has sowed seeds of disillusionment and has given birth to a new cynicism. For example, recently the largest foundations of the country were invited to send representatives to a national meeting called by the chairman of the Inter-Agency Committee on Mexican-American Affairs.[16] The hope was entertained that these foundations, after hearing of the problems, would become involved in the concerns of Mexican-Americans in the United States. This conference was a total failure. Not a single foundation was represented at the conference, and most even neglected to send regrets.[17]

12. *As the Child Reads . . . : The Treatment of Minorities in Textbooks and Other Teaching Materials*, National NEA-PR&R Conference on Civil and Human Rights in Education (Washington, D.C., February 8–10, 1967), pp. 4, 11.

13. Charles C. Cumberland, "The United States-Mexican Border: A Selective Guide to the Literature of the Region," Supplement to *Rural Sociology*, vol. 25, no. 2, June 1960.

14. David K. Gast, "Characteristics and Concepts of Minority Americans in Contemporary Children's Functional Literature" (Ed.D. dissertation, Arizona State University, 1965).

15. Mark M. Krug, "History Textbooks in England and in the United States," *Elementary English*, December 1963, pp. 821–824.

16. Conference called by the Honorable Vicente Ximenes, Chairman of the Committee, U.S. Office of Education, Department of Health, Education and Welfare, Washington, D.C.

17. "Foundations Snub Mexican-Americans," *San Jose Mercury*, April 2, 1969.

The current situation can be summarized this way. The most recent assessments of printed matter used in schools find that *the great fault of contemporary publications is the omission* of accounts of Mexican-Americans and related historical events. Where older and discontinued books are in use, especially as "enrichment and supplemental" reading, the older negative stereotypes are reinforced.

If educators are to serve in a leadership capacity, they should be in the forefront demanding textbook content revision. One way to get new and, hopefully, better texts is through a major curriculum reform in all subject areas.[18] This reform would require totally new texts, especially in the social sciences and humanities. The first step, however, is to become aware of the deficits and to insist on the proper kind of literature for educational use.

## BIBLIOGRAPHY

BILLINGTON, RAY ALLEN. "Bias in History Textbooks." *Saturday Review* 49, January 15, 1966, pp. 59–61, 80–81.

ROBINSON, DONALD W., ed. *As Others See Us: International Views of American History*. Boston: Houghton Mifflin Co., 1969, p. 2.

WOLFE, MANSELL WAYNE. "The Images of the United States in the Hispanic American Press: A Content Analysis of News and Opinions of This Country Appearing in Daily Newspapers from Nineteen American Republics." Ph.D. dissertation, Indiana University, 1963.

18. The process of revision does not mean the distortion of facts, lessening the truth, or compromises.

# chapter 3

# Education

No general discussion about Mexican-Americans is complete without at least recognizing the role of formal education. Increasingly, more and more Mexican-American youth are successfully completing secondary schools. Education increases in acceptance among Mexican-American youth as it becomes a realistic vehicle for reaching future goals; yet too many youth today, for personal as well as societal reasons, continue to drop out. The solution to this social failure is a task for concerted professional and community application.

The number of high school graduates continuing to colleges and universities is far too limited, and encouraging these young people and facilitating their entry into post-high-school education and training are major tasks ahead.

The section which follows expresses some concerns about education as related to Mexican-Americans. Fuller discussions of issues, programs, and philosophies may be found in other sources.[1]

Even a casual inspection of achievement indexes for Mexican-Americans in most communities shows that considerable vertical mobility is taking place. Rather than being handed advantages by their families, these Mexican-Americans have made it the hard way. And education has been, and promises to continue to be, the principal tool for the improvement of personal and family well-being. Other factors undoubtedly enter into any achievement story, but this does not diminish the strategic role of education.

Almost no attention is given to these subgroups which quietly and unpretentiously compete successfully in the American system. Understandably, the

---

1. Herschel T. Manuel, *Spanish-speaking Children of the Southwest* (Austin: University of Texas Press, 1965); Julian Samora, "The Education of the Spanish-speaking in the Southwest" (Paper, January 13, 1963); George I. Sanchez, "Spanish in the Southwest," Occidental College, April 6, 1963; L. S. Tireman, *Teaching Spanish-Speaking Children*, rev. ed. (Albuquerque: University of New Mexico Press, 1951).

disadvantages of more than fifty percent of the ethnic group have commanded recent attention from individuals as well as groups of Anglo-Americans and Chicanos. No mincing of words can be justified in describing this exclusion of the poor. The need is real and requires understanding and mass effort before marked improvement can be stabilized.

Accepting the substantial achievement by some, many Mexican-Americans are still poorly served by the public schools and higher education institutions. Those people or agencies responsible for the implementation of educational programs cannot escape the full onus for their failure with these Mexican-American children who are bilingual, bicultural, and further alienated from the American culture. At the same time, in searching for the roots of the problem it is naïve to lay the full blame on education. Clearly the needs of Mexican-Americans should be served by other social institutions, but this does not happen. Observed deficiencies are interrelated with what happens with politics, jobs, income, housing, recreation, and opportunities. Education is still the prime agent, however, for the alleviation of many of these shortcomings.

In discussing action for progress, oversimplifications about biculturalism and bilingualism lessen the probability of clear success in school and community programs.

A growing number of children come from homes where parents are a mixed marriage and their offspring cannot be categorized as bicultural or bilingual children. English is the only language spoken either in the home or in the immediate environment prior to and during enrollment in school. This is also true for a growing number of children whose parents are both of Mexican descent. These children and families are rather fully acculturated into the mainstream and respond favorably to the going system of value orientations. Many children and families appear to feel no sense of alienation or self-doubt about their ethnicity. Errors are compounded, therefore, to equate these young with those children who indeed may be recent immigrants or with those who have remained isolated from the Anglo community and have made lesser inroads into the acculturative stream. When this is the case, modifications and flexibility are needed in programming for Mexican-descent children. Regrettably, almost no research is available which describes acculturated Mexican-American children.

Average statistics presenting educational and social achievement of many Mexican-American children show clearly that the achievement average is below the norms in many school subjects. The greatest toll takes place in those measurements which require verbal responses and understanding of concepts especially foreign to the culture of the child. The enormity of this situation requires dramatic action. The failure of the educational program in school is paralleled by the marginality of these children's families in the total socioeconomic community. These families tend to be chronically poor by measures of family income, occupation, and mobility. Economic hardships are real and constant, and total disaster is the wolf always at the door. This is the home background poor children bring to class with them.

Noting the many denials of the rewards of the system to Mexican-Americans, questions must be raised about basic causes. Few argue today that the system has rejected and failed this group. Employment and educational opportunities tend to be limited chiefly for ethnic and culture differences, yet questions are also raised today about the total accuracy of this explanation. Some observers say that the suppressed socioeconomic condition of the group is essentially explained by the culture of poverty construct. These particular families exhibit characteristics most generally found in poor people the world over. More research is needed before this can be answered to everyone's satisfaction.

Educational needs are continuous throughout every level of schooling. It is necessary, however, to note that preschool education is probably the crucial priority for these very poor if they are to achieve at a level consistent with their innate intelligence and talents and with a performance quality which will enable them to compete successfully later in the world of work. Formal school programs intervening between preschool and higher education must certainly be reformed in order to serve those Mexican-Americans excluded to this date. Simply stated, these reorganizations can take the form of multicultural approaches to learning and the incorporation of new instructional materials. Innovative teaching procedures are important for all children as well as Mexican-Americans. The present state of research supports the conclusion that no one teaching method exists that is better suited for Mexican-Americans any more than for anyone else. This is true of materials as well. Individual differences in learning must be recognized. For individuals functioning at the frontiers of the Anglo-American culture and language, changes in curricular organization are basic and bilingual education concepts become key.

An accurate estimate of a child's ability is at the heart of creating an educational program that will nurture his talent. School assessments are notoriously poor for many children of Mexican descent. When children are from low socioeconomic families, as well as being ethnically different, errors of judgment are often great.[2]

2. Ninety-five percent of the children placed in the EMR (Educable Mentally Retarded) classes in a Santa Clara County (Calif.) school district are Mexican-Americans. This statistic clearly shows either a lack of professional integrity or an ignorance about expected rates of incidence of mental retardation in humans. Neither condition is forgivable in professionals.

Multicultural programs in schools may be one way to minimize this error in judgment. They may also meet a national and international urgency and be the means by which the child identifies with the history, literature, explorations, and personalities that give life to America. The self-worth of the child may be nurtured with a multicultural approach which also contributes to improved human relations and the acceptance of diverse peoples and their cultures. This educational program can become, then, an organization for maintaining and enlarging skills and learnings about the mother culture as well as a means for developing the individual's skills in English and other basic learnings important for success. Not to achieve the latter is to insure continued exclusion of the individual from full participation in society.

The success of comprehensive bilingual and multicultural educational programs can only be attained if new criteria of success are defined. Educators and communities must come to grips with the question of traditional standards and measures of achievement in many areas of instruction. New talents and abilities must be recognized and valued. Means for evaluating these other abilities must be constructed and this measurement system incorporated in or replace the present one which now serves as a basis for promotions and other rewards of the system. Educators have talked about but have not yet made the commitment to restudy and revise their criteria of success, and until they do, the true value of bilingual education or multicultural programs for all children cannot be appreciated.

Mexican-Americans in large numbers object to the common grouping in elementary schools and tracking practices found in junior and senior high schools over the country. In spite of the theoretical possibility that children may move from one group to another and from one track to another, a child once placed in a special program or a given track will tend to stay there. In this organizational rigidity, it is far more common for him to regress than to progress. It is a sad but true commentary that, proportionately, too many Mexican-Americans are assigned to the lowest and least-esteemed curriculum tracks. These children really have no place to go. Little wonder that lack of motivation, where it exists, tends to remain a problem for all teachers to "overcome." With understandable reason Chicano militants demand that tracking systems and all the paraphernalia which support them, such as standard tests and testing programs, be discarded at once.

Past studies consistently find that Mexican-American children beginning in the first grade slip in school achievement in comparison to Anglo-American school norms. Actually, in most studies differences tend to be minimal while the children are in the primary grades, but the educational fiasco begins to rear its ugly head for these children approximately in the fourth grade. By the time they are in high school, those who are left, many are so far behind in achievement that they are simply custodial cases, and having no good reason for staying, they can hardly wait for any pretext to leave. Degrees of drop-out vary from sixty to ninety percent in some studies. Considering educational strategies, concerned people emphasize the importance of the early years of childhood—though the intervening school years cannot be written off as nonproductive.

A commonality of language, social, and informal learning experiences are starting points in the conventional learning process for the majority of Anglo-American children. Mexican-American children coming from poverty-prone families not effectively in the mainstream of America can be expected to start and, unless intervention strategies are effective, to continue at a disadvantage. Poverty takes its toll, too, of disadvantaged Anglo-American children.

Recognizing these inequities in the educational process, school people and communities have two alternatives theoretically open. Schools may restructure programs so that culture learning, the Spanish language, and innate talents of Mexican-American children become assets rather than liabilities. Instructional programs start with the Mexican-American child where he is. Bilingual education, of course, is one way to achieve this state and benefits both Mexican-American and Anglo alike. The other alternative is to provide enriched environment and experiences which will supply the culture and basic learnings as well as language which other children from English-language and middle-class homes already possess. In most instances, this is what the preschool programs such as Project Headstart have attempted to achieve.[3]

Using the culture of the child as a springboard is conceptually promising. Yet at this moment studies incorporating this notion and with a design that permits credible assessment are scarce, so conclusions are based on hopes rather than proof, and much needs to be ascertained about the validity of this speculation. Giving support to this approach are the misgivings attached to forcing a child to suppress his own culture in the process of learning exclusively the Anglo-American culture.

Polarizations arise on these issues. How are these two simple questions of preschool program models resolved when the majority of Mexican-American children lie somewhere in between the poles of Mexican and Anglo-American languages and cultures? Except for the severely socially

---

3. A few extremists denounce Project Headstart as subversive for the Mexican-American child. This objection is essentially based on misinformation; based on its present rationale this objection should be rejected. The *one* educational strategy, if such a choice were possible, with the greatest potential for children from marginal families— but not necessarily from all Mexican-American families—is an early and sustained preschool program with close involvement by school and community.

isolated and the most recent immigrant, perhaps, no Mexican-American child has escaped degrees of enculturation.

Carefully designed language and bilingual education studies and reports are too few, infrequent, and inconclusive. Variations in bilingual education experience and their effect on self-identity and acceptance are not yet reliably tested in the changing tides of educational programs. Much opinion is expressed in strong support for the merits of bilingual education. The hope that greater progress can be achieved in basic learnings and in self-esteem if schools do begin with the child's culture and language explains the attraction of this program.

While other cultures may serve as starting points in learning in American schools, it is reasonable to expect the Anglo-American culture and its characteristics will continue dominant in the United States. Anyone who wishes to share in the fruits of the system as they are currently valued must be able to function effectively within this system. This means enabling a person to have effective command or access to the political, economic, and educational resources of the society. This view in no way detracts from the notion that America is a pluralistic nation, and differing culture groups are able to flourish side by side, sharing together culture elements borrowed from each other and all thriving the richer for this cultural interaction.

Mexican-American activists for years have challenged schools, colleges, and universities. Teachers, administrators, and professors are rebuked for their preoccupation with narrow academic and teaching specialties and for their insensitivity to the Spanish-speaking minorities. Whatever the rationalization today for the failure of these institutions and personnel, it cannot be because voices are subdued today. Protests and demands are loud, harsh, and disrespectful. Militants say, "We cannot wait. *Es tiempo.*"

The insistence for educational opportunities is for more than mere entry to conventional programs. For pragmatic as well as ideologic reasons, it is also a demand for ethnic studies. This cry is raised uniformly at colleges and universities wherever *La Raza* is found in numbers. Spokesmen throughout the Southwest repeatedly argue the imperative to establish an identity. This identity is ethnic in orientation, and the vehicle for the resurrection is restructured and innovative curriculums.

This search for Mexican-American identity heightens emotional reactions toward institutions charged with dereliction. Because an understanding and an empathic faculty are basic for the initiation of required changes, a high emphasis is placed on teachers who are ethnic individuals. Who can better understand the bilingual and bicultural uniqueness of Mexican-Americans? Who knows the problems of marginal students better than those who have also suffered—but survived—shortcomings of the system? Who but a Chicano teacher, counselor, or administrator can interpret better the subjectives of historical confrontations between Anglos and Mexicans along the expansive Rio Grande and elsewhere?

These arguments rest on the simplicity of the supposition that the ethnic group is indeed monolithic in cultural nature. Much can be said with justice and validity for this assumption. But in its all-inclusiveness it is too naïve to be appropriate but for a small fraction. This gross simplicity does not attempt to consider essential questions such as, Are all Mexican-Americans equally acculturated or alienated? Do they all speak English and Spanish? If so in what degrees? Are the needs and future goals all of the same nature, and can they all be satisfied by ethnic studies as such? Are all individuals crippled by a sense of inferiority and if not is there a total need to restore identity? Is it essential that all Chicanos be required to take these programs? Obviously no one answer can be established for such searchings and others like them. For the good of these ethnic programs basic questions and others need to be raised and examined critically.

Questions of this nature raised by a few have been disregarded at the moment by noisy militants, ultraliberals, and pragmatic administrators.[4] Honest questions and fully explored answers are prerequisites to the conceptual foundations of those courses which will best serve Mexican-Americans. Surely Mexican-American studies have as much justification as any other scholarly division. In this instance it is well to consider that it is not an *Anglo-American* or a *Mexican* studies center that is sought, but rather *Mexican-American*. The germane question to be answered is "What are Mexican-American studies?" Certainly they are not a mere cataloging of course titles. Ethnic studies deserve the full commitment from educational institutions in personnel, financing, resources, and long-range development of programs that have goals of professional and scholarly dimensions.

Any viable rationale for ethnic studies in the America of today, in addition to offering courses and experiences of valid substance to the minority students themselves, must have value for Anglo-Americans. And it can be said that this attribute, something of value for all America, is one of the conceptual strengths of ethnic studies. It is crucial for twentieth-century Americans to get rid of nineteenth-century perspectives. American society is the creation of peoples from many lands, and the beauty and vitality of the achievements of these immigrants are thoroughly integral aspects of America, even though the Puritan Ethic and the influence of the original central European culture are pervasive.

But today the Third World is very much a part of events, and the future of America may well be decided by the ability of Anglo-Americans to live

4. It is difficult to estimate the harm to long-reaching constructive curriculum development by administrators primarily motivated to avoid conflict at any cost. Essentially, they are conceding that programs for Mexican-Americans are of no consequence.

harmoniously and productively with the many cultured and languaged groups of the earth. Ethnic studies have the ingredients and potential for these learnings right at home, and Anglo-American students may be the first to enjoy the fruits of these programs.

If research institutions are to be censured, it is for their avoidance of study and research about Mexican-Americans. This reproach in no way negates the contributions of individuals distinguished as scholars and pioneers in the study of Mexican-Americans. But universities and colleges are to be indicted. The many who are critical and impatient over the insistence of the strident voices of the minorities for change must remember that because authority was unresponsive to the moderate voices in the past, new voices are now raised.

The place of the new ethnic studies within the traditional academic institutions is not clear at this moment, but hopes are high. Certainly it is an approved addition to the multiple offerings in a growing number of educational institutions; beyond that it is conjecture. A pecking order in the disciplines has long existed in academia as well as in secondary education, and ethnic studies can expect a "respectability" rating to emerge. The academic competence, credentials, and integrity of the initiators will influence strongly the status accorded to the program by peers.

Basically, ethnic studies need to consider two major student target groups. Obviously, ethnic studies will serve Chicano youth. Some of these may well use the program for entry and continuation in educational programs leading toward occupational and personal goals. Some individuals will search for identity and self-esteem, and the studies may support this regeneration. Others more at ease with the world will be challenged by the new vistas and will gain a sense of fulfillment in exploring and discovering the roots of the mother culture. And for personal reasons, some students may seek and need only a light exposure, if any at all, to the formalized experiences of the studies.

The other target, of course, is the Anglo-American student group— more aptly the target becomes *all* other students. The value of these studies was previously cited and will contribute to goals of interethnic respect and acceptance which are essentials for any long-range and enduring gains in relationships between the varied groups. Another argument less sanguine but very American in its pragmatism exists for these ethnic studies. Generally, Anglo-Americans are beneficiaries of an ascribed status with certain privileges. If they, speaking of the total generational hierarchy, occupy at least for the moment key positions at all levels of the system, then constructive change in attitude and behavior within the majority group—along with internal gains by Mexican-American groups—can be expected ultimately to affect the rate and nature of opportunities throughout the entire spectrum of the cultural society. In other words, artificial barriers existing because people do not understand and respect each other will be reduced.

Some Mexican-Americans will specialize in ethnic studies, and they will be needed for teaching these courses in schools.[5] It may be expected that most Mexican-Americans in higher education will continue to choose studies in other fields leading to occupational and professional objectives. This is probably inevitable, but it is also completely desirable. A few will need the catharsis of emotional release while they truly search for an identity with which they can live.

Ethnic studies must be available as a free choice for all Mexican-Americans. The majority of them in higher education may seek only a few foundation courses; they really have no identity problem. If ethnic studies courses also satisfy other higher education-general education requirements, then choosing basic courses in these programs will be simplified for all students. If the studies are also successful in attracting and influencing the thinking and behavior of majority students, their creation will be doubly justified.

Realistically, Mexican-American students, along with knowing themselves, will best serve the needs of the ethnic group by penetrating scholarly, professional, and technological occupations as quickly and as thoroughly as possible. This is a necessary condition in a contemporary society. This view is basic if the goal for Mexican-Americans is sharing in and contributing to the cultural as well as the economic and political domains of America to the degree that the individual chooses without any external impediment. It is believed that this is the goal.

5. Implications to the education of Mexican-American children if all Anglo teachers received a solid Chicano ethnic studies background exhilarate the imagination.

# chapter 4

# Health and Conflict

Migrants following the seasonal work trails face serious health hazards. The wide-open spaces and the endless roads or rural backways are too often journeys without shelter from the cold or the heat. Hitting the road is a line of march without rest camps, baths, toilets, or comfort. Pauses are for quick bites of the most filling and the cheapest food, and then on with the search for work, somewhere—a job which merely enables these migrants, Mexican-Americans and others, to repeat the dead-end cycle of futility once again.

Disproportionately, Mexican-Americans are found among America's 26 million poor. All the handicaps and denials found in poverty groups apply to these poor, especially if they are engaged in seasonal agricultural work, and it is this visible distress that makes them appear so different to the bathed and well-fed middle class. A convenient myth flourishes that the poor in America are childishly happy in their poverty. This is convenient because it assuages the feelings of guilt and it supports a sense of moral righteousness. The aches and pains of these poor are presumed to be less; that by choice they prefer a simple, monotonous, and low-cost diet. Most felicitously the poor escape the price of middleclassism—the psychosomatic afflictions and tensions created by keeping up with the Joneses.

Health data on the poor strain credulity. The facts are that the poor are incapacitated and confined to bed twice as often as the nonpoor. Major disabilities such as heart disease, arthritis, hypertension, and visual defects afflict the poor four times as often as the nonpoor. Mothers and babies die in childbirth more often or fail to survive in greater numbers.[1]

Doctors available to the *barrio* or the migrant camps or the hard-core ghettos are less than half of those available to the rest of the community. Health facilities and services are frequently inferior. The poor and the entire

---

1. *Health Wanted: For Millions of Americans*, a preliminary report from the Health Task Force of The Urban Coalition (Washington, D.C.: The Urban Coalition, 1819 H. Street, N.W.), July 1969.

society suffer because so little in preventive medical services reaches the Mexican-American and other poor. The loss to society is great because the talents and contributions are effectively reduced.

The national shortage of medical personnel and services severely affects those areas where Mexican-American poor are concentrated. In their *barrios* and migrant camps the incidence of tuberculosis, poor dental hygiene, and alcoholism, for example, are greater than in the community at large. The recognized shortage of personnel and facilities compounded by the cultural and communications barriers are major obstacles to adequate health care. Though many programs are needed to solve this problem, a wholesale recruitment of medical aides with some medical training, while not a final answer to the shortage, could complement available medical services in these communities. Such services could also offer paraprofessional training and occupations.

In the urban *barrio* many Mexican-Americans are dependent on unskilled employment. Many are commuters to agricultural areas, returning to their homes at night. In the *barrios* of the poor and migrant camps, illness, disease, and infestations often run their course in cycles. People suffer, not because they are fatalistic, but rather because they are powerless to alter the course of events.

Rural health problems are raised almost routinely for public notice every year. Individuals, often sensitive professionals, fail to stir apathetic professional medical groups, communities, and public officials who too often respond more to political expediency rather than moral conscience.

The health problems in one of the richest agricultural counties in the nation serve to illustrate the problem.[2] During irrigation periods many of the *barrios* along creeks and artesian wells are flooded and mosquitoes plague the community. Pesticides are used in the orchards without enforcement of safety regulations by the authorities. The reason for this laxness is never well explained. One medical practitioner reported that in this area 100 to 200 county farm workers suffer each year from pesticide poisoning. He objected to the lack of enforcement of pesticide rules.

A different doctor in the community when confronted with the health problem expressed a pride in the effectiveness of the hospitals. He believed the hospitals, as well as the doctors' offices, were open to all regardless of economic means. A Mexican-American housewife expressed a *barrio* sentiment by saying that the *bolillos* (gringos) do not understand the embarrassment Mexicans feel when they are unable to pay their doctor bills. This reaction contradicts the viewpoint of a county social welfare worker who asserted that Mexican people are really very happy people.

2. *San Francisco Chronicle*, June 30, 1969.

A former state director of public health in California summed the situation tersely by saying it is impossible for people to have good health without decent food, decent housing, pure water, jobs, and education.

Concerns are expressed repeatedly over the health problems of the poor and the Mexican-American minority; yet according to a recent report from the School of Public Health at the University of California at Los Angeles, almost *no data* exist on health services for Mexican-Americans and the utilization of these services.[3] As noted previously, too often social services and personnel are not available. Under these conditions Mexican-Americans have little choice but to draw upon known resources and traditions. And why not! The *curandero*, the herbs, are better than no treatment.

Though isolated physically and socially in many instances from the majority community, Mexican-Americans are clearly aware that America boasts of the most advanced medical techniques of the world. But they also know that this medical knowledge and these laboratory skills are not available to the large numbers of Mexican-Americans among the poor. The poor are the first victims of this neglect.

Though affluent, this America ranks thirteenth in the world in infant mortality and at least that high in maternal deaths.[4] The reduction of health disabilities in the United States is a problem of major proportions. Over five and one-half million Americans are mentally ill; one out of five children suffers from a chronic ailment; at least four million children are classified as mentally retarded (Mexican-American children are disproportionately assigned to special classes); one out of four persons will have cancer; over fifteen million persons have a heart disease; no less than twelve million are victims of arthritis; and four out of five elderly suffer from chronic illness.[5]

Diets of the poor are deficient. A high incidence of nutritional anemia is frequently found among Mexican-American adults and children from low-income areas. Food habits are tenacious in their struggle for cultural survival, and *frijoles*, *arroz*, *maíz*, and *tortillas* are common menu items. Yet beans, rice, corn, and tortillas are too much starch if not supplemented with green vegetables and protein. Those are staples in the diets of poor Mexican-Americans because they are cheap, tasty, and filling.[6]

In small communities farm workers are easily spotted, but this is not the case in urban areas. Here farm workers lose their identity and are ignored, though nationwide public programs are directed toward the needs

3. "The Mexican-American" (Paper prepared for the U.S. Commission on Civil Rights, 1968).
4. Ibid.
5. *New York Times*, December 31, 1968.
6. Dra. Blanca Ordoñez, Assistant Chief of Preventive Medicine, Social Security Institute of Mexico City, in *Christian Science Monitor*, August 22, 1969.

of seasonal agricultural workers. Mexican-Americans who work on farms are chiefly urban dwellers. Eighty-five percent of the Spanish-surname population of California, for example, live in urban areas. At the same time, the majority of the farm workers continue to be Mexican-descent people. All the problems of the rural poor face these urban farm workers: poor health, substandard housing, unemployment, economic deprivation, and discrimination. Each of these alone is a major crisis, but combined they are chaotic calamities.

Differences in the perception of illness are to be found within the ethnic group. Geographic areas and generational differences are part of the explanation. Many Mexican-Americans in Texas, for example, especially along the Rio Grande border, have resisted many elements of the Anglo way of life. In other instances there are no differences.

One study of folk societal traditions classified five distinct illnesses among the border Mexican-Americans. These were described as (1) *caída de la mollera* (fallen fontanel), (2) *empacho* (food blocking the intestinal tract), (3) *mal ojo* (evil eye), (4) *susto* (shock), and (5) *mal puesto* (sorcery).[7] Though folk medicine practices were observed, the project staff was aware that health and treatment beliefs are changing. Some patients ask for modern medical treatment and at the same time solicit *curandero* services and use folk remedies.

These folk beliefs are devalued today by Mexican-Americans oriented toward dominant culture values. These beliefs are regarded as naïve, yet even the most anglicized Mexican-American encounters within his extended family group some individuals who are believers in folk medicine. Every sizable Mexican-American community has its "Mexican" store where, in addition to staples and hardware, advice and the common herbs used for home treatment may be found.[8]

A few cities develop health programs in *barrios*.[9] One urban center stated these specific objectives in their program: (1) to raise the immuniza-

7. Fred R. Crawford, *The Forgotten Egg: A Study of the Mental Health Problems of Mexican-American Residents of the Good Samaritan Center* (Austin, Tex.: Division of Mental Health, Texas State Department of Health © 1961), p. 5. Refer also to: Margaret Clark, *Health in the Mexican-American Culture* (Berkeley: University of California Press, 1959); William Madsen, *The Mexican-Americans of South Texas* (New York: Holt, Rinehart and Winston, Inc., 1964); Arthur J. Rubel, *Across the Tracks: Mexican-Americans in a Texas City* (Austin: University of Texas Press, 1966); Lyle Saunders, *Cultural Differences and Medical Care: Case of the Spanish-Speaking People of the Southwest* (New York: Russell Sage Foundation, 1954).

8. Luis G. Cabrera, *Plantas Curatives de México: Propiedades Medicinales de las Más Conocidas Plantas de México su Aplicación Correcta y Eficaz*, Quinto Edición (Edición Ciceron, Mexico, D.F., 1958).

9. The inadequate prenatal care, dietary deficiencies, and poor health, according to medical research, explain the greater incidence of mental retardation among the very poor. Intelligence tests standardized on WASP norms and used indiscriminately are also culturally biased against many Mexican-Americans.

tion level of preschool-age children and adults residing in the area, (2) to raise the number of expectant mothers utilizing prenatal services at the county hospital, (3) to increase the use of other health and welfare resources by residents of the area, (4) to minimize the fragmentation of health and welfare services by stimulating communication among agency personnel providing service in the area, and (5) to encourage the development of indigenous leadership which can articulate the needs of the residents in the area.[10] While health problems of the poor among Mexican-Americans must be perceived, it is also clear that substantial numbers of Mexican-Americans are operating at the same level of American mores and practices in health care.

If health programs such as the one cited are to make an impact, strong fiscal support, basic resources, and continuity of programs must be provided. Health impairment continues to be a critical problem in rural and agricultural areas throughout much of the Southwest. This is a social negligence on the part of authorities and communities which can be corrected.

Condescension is a familiar posture of the dominant community about Mexican folk medicine practices. A thinly disguised humor is at times apparent when the cultural values or reasons for *mal ojo*, for instance, are elaborated. Frequently a sense of disbelief is sensed when families who have lived in the United States for many generations reveal that some health beliefs they speak about or are aware of fall into the category of folk medicinal practices.

Yet, while displaying a stance of superiority on matters of health practices, the majority-group person overlooks the veil of tradition and community culture practices woven around the Anglo doctor-patient relationship. Often the doctor performs a traditional ritual but actually permits nature to perform the curative function. Or he may only alleviate the discomfort. The wags make the common cold a good example of this: "If you go to a doctor for treatment you'll get well in a week; if you let the cold run its course you'll recover in seven days."

In orthodox practice today, some practitioners are critical of hasty surgery as a way to combat health problems. The body will frequently recuperate if left alone. Few ridicule excessive use of surgery, and it maintains an aura of scientific respectability.

Popular myth holds that the poor are happy, are satisfied with their lot, and are spared the anguish of mental or psychological disorders, and the affluent, under the inner tensions of vertical mobility, solicit the services of the tribal medicine men—the psychoanalyst, therapist, the psychiatrist.[11]

10. "Seasonal Farm Worker Report," San Jose (Calif.) City Health Department, 1964.
11. Ben H. Bagdikian, *In the Midst of Plenty* (New York: The New American Library Inc., Signet Books, 1964); Michael Harrington, *The Other America: Poverty in the U.S.* (Baltimore, Md.: Penguin Books, Inc., 1962).

Further, after submitting to the mumbo jumbo of the ritual, these middle-class patients feel they have gained status symbols. Society fails to consider that these medicine men, no matter what the apprenticeship, are pursuing similar "tribal rituals" and are using mystic rites in the treatment and recovery process of the victim. The curative value of faith healing is not really different.

For some, the affluence of America is an amoral dimension; not so for Mexican-Americans. Science has made the heart transplant possible; yet *most of the world poor die of the most simple diseases.* In the United States forty percent of the population falls below the poverty line in income. An emerging view in the United States today is that

> We believe that one of the marks of a humane and good society is reasonably equal access to health services for all people. . . . This value has come to be considered a basic human right beyond dispute in principle.
> . . . The social system itself generated diseases and that only by changing the social system and human behavior patterns quite drastically can we hope to reduce the incidence of certain diseases.[12]

Until the professionals as well as total communities muster to the common cause, disease and disability will continue rampant among those who, like migrant Mexican-Americans, continue to survive on the fringe of an affluent society.

12. Odin W. Anderson, *Health Services in a Land of Plenty,* Health Administration Perspectives No. A7 (University of Chicago, 1968), pp. 61, 75.

# chapter 5

# The Housing Crisis

Growing numbers of Mexican-Americans live in comfortable urban and suburban homes. Studies have not been completed which indicate the number of Mexican-Americans who are middle class and who now live in the better neighborhoods. But it is economic reality to recognize that better homes require a financial ability not found among the low-income groups whatever the ethnic origin. Mexican-Americans are employed in growing numbers in trade unions and blue-collar jobs. They are employees of governmental and local agencies in semiprofessional and professional occupations. They are self-employed in business and professional categories. Consequently, these individuals are in a position to make reasonable choices about the quality of home and location of neighborhood in which they wish to live.

Totally free selection of homes, according to some reports, may be limited at times because of prejudices or discrimination, but this tends to be a covert experience rather than an obvious phenomenon today for those at this higher socioeconomic level. Bluntly speaking, the discrimination that exists in housing today is most exactingly directed against the poor and disadvantaged Mexican-American. People intimately acquainted with Mexican-Americans know of the discrimination some have experienced, especially in their efforts to find rental or to lease houses.

Too many Mexican-Americans today fall into the "poor" category and continue to live in substandard housing. This housing ranges from the most dilapidated shelters found in rural areas to the substandard dwellings especially abundant in aging urban centers. In varying degrees, these constructions may be without electricity, water, plumbing, lighting, ventilation, and other features required for wholesome living. Frequently these homes are overcrowded. They are too expensive for the poor who have no real choice in selection from the housing market.

Housing experts estimate that under normal conditions a family should not exceed more than twenty percent of its annual income on housing. A family earning $3,000 a year should budget $50 a month housing. The high cost of real estate and high rentals make this a practical impossibility. Consequently, the poor are forced to pay greater proportions of their total income on housing. Crowding in with other family members and the sharing of costs are the only economies possible.

America takes pride in its middle-class symbols, but it ignores the needs of those without decent housing, furnishings, clothing, recreation, and other physical and social needs. Issues of deficient housing—some experts state that America is a nation of substandard and inadequate housing—are hushed or fail to receive affirmative action. A classic establishment tactic is to refer problems to ad hoc study committees. Of course, this is a reasonable procedure, but it may also become a tactic to gain time and to place obstacles in the way of accomplishing anything requiring an investment of resources. It also forces impatient people to give up in disillusionment. Vocal protesters, too, may perhaps be encouraged to go away. It is the Anglo game of *mañana*. Action may never come.

Suburbanites often do not want to be bothered with housing needs of others. In the long run, however, this view is a shortsighted investment because eventually the community must face these social deficiencies and the expense may be greater.

Bad housing affects all humans directly and indirectly. It cripples the lives of those who live in it as well as others in the total community. Recently a young Mexican-American mother and two small children, ejected from temporary housing, were forced to spend the night under a bridge. Humane communities cannot tolerate this kind of situation.

Some of the ill-effects of bad housing are (1) poor health as a result of unsafe construction, dirt and filth, rats and vermin, (2) depressing effect on children from inadequate or nonexisting play or recreation facilities, and exposure to danger and injury, (3) privacy needs at a premium from living continuously in overcrowded houses, (4) deteriorating neighborhoods with insufficient and inadequate community facilities, hospitals, schools, and stores, (5) excessive distances from work locations which hurt the total family, (6) the way people feel about themselves—loss of self-respect, and (7) conflict between tenants and landlord which also contributes to antisocial attitudes.

While some Mexican-Americans live in decent housing, the great majority do not. Those who suffer the most over this matter are the ones least able to make changes in their ability to earn or to determine where they will live. These people are the powerless in America.

People are poor because they do not have money—this is no penetrating conclusion. Most of the funds in America for the construction of dwellings come from the private sector of the economy, and there is always a means test which effectively keeps the poor out. The government tends to facilitate the flow of money through guarantees, but the actual money comes from banks, savings and loan associations, and corporate investors such as insurance companies. Any program facing the needs of housing for poor Mexican-Americans must take these realities into account.

Other problems face the poor in their scramble for housing. Community action programs to provide aid or guidance to groups must face issues such as (1) landlord conflicts and eviction notices which are a worry for many poor, (2) emergency repairs of the house which become pressing problems because older homes are in a constant state of disrepair, and (3) problems of relocation in urban areas. Where do the poor go when they are displaced by the construction of a freeway or an urban development project? What provisions are made so that the family does not lose all contacts and former friends? How are these families helped in the search for housing? Who can help? These are questions confronting each city.

Middle-class workers in housing programs often are not personally acquainted with problems of unsanitary or overcrowded housing. Others who have improved their economic lot may have forgotten what it is like to be poor. Those with no choice do not forget and are only too well aware of the deficiencies.

Outsiders frequently see a Mexican-American *barrio* in a farming community as something romantic. The people look different. The food is exotic. The Spanish language is always musical in sound. Neighborhood stores with their herbs and chile and Mexican pastry have a warm human quality often lacking in downtown's business district. For the Mexican-American this is home. Here everything is familiar; his family, friends, and *compadres* are always around to lend support. But the native resident is also aware of the differences between the *barrio* and the Anglo-American middle-class suburbs.

Frequently the *barrio* is characterized by low-cost substandard homes. Often it is a fringe residential section of a larger community. City services are often limited, and if the area is unincorporated, police and fire protection come from the county or the forestry department. The *barrio* is isolated and neglected by city or county authorities.

In rural migrant camps the available water supply may be inadequate and contaminated. All families in a migrant worker camp may use the same water tap, toilets, washing and bathing facilities. In some nonincorporated areas, the water mains and pipes do not prevent contamination from outhouses, cesspools, and uncontrolled disposal of waste and trash. Where Mexican nationals or those who enter illegally are hired for farm work, the available housing for resident families becomes scarcer.

What do the poor ask?[1] They want "a house with running water." "Toilets to use. . . ." "Not having to live on the ditch bank." In other words they want what all families want—decent housing. An aerial survey of the agricultural area clearly showed that many "migrant families occupied the banks of the Kings River and bunched together in makeshift field camps. . . ." This was also true of other areas. Conspicuous needs for migrant family housing during flash peak seasons are for inexpensive adequate units, such as the "paradome" or "plydom," which include water and sewage services.

Whether urban or rural dwellings, homes need adequate kitchen facilities, heating equipment, light and ventilation for all rooms, and enough space for the family to eliminate overcrowdedness. Yet cheap adequate housing is seldom available where it is most needed.

Humanitarians recognize the harmful effects of poor housing. Families become disoriented and in conflict with society. School no matter how good cannot combat the cumulative deficits of early deprivations from deficient neighborhoods. It is clear that great numbers of Mexican-Americans require decent low-cost housing. Attractive and decent environment and basic services must be within reach of all the poor.

Housing shortages for Mexican-American poor reflect the need for low-cost decent housing for all American poor in urban and rural areas. The debate about low-cost housing rages, programs are announced periodically, and no results are evident. Typical of public reaction to the unavailability of low-cost housing are the following:

Affluent Santa Clara County is mired in a severe housing crisis that hurts the poor . . . and creates segregation and ghettos. It is . . . driving the affluent and poor, and the Anglo-Saxon majority and the Mexican-American minority farther and farther apart. . . . There has been an increasing inability of the housing market to respond to the needs of low income households. (Louis Barba, Acting President of the National Association of Home Builders, by Jim Choate, in *San Jose Mercury*, California, January 8, 1970).

The government increase in the maximum interest rate for FHA and GI home loan mortgages from 7.5 and 8.5 percent (effective January 5, 1970) . . . would boost monthly costs to buyers, disqualify more buyers on an income basis, serve to raise rents, and tend to reduce housing available. . . . (Santa Clara County Planning Department Study in *San Jose Mercury*, California, December 31, 1969).

Currently, a family must earn approximately $12,000 a year if it is to have reasonable expectation for home ownership. (*Sun*, Milpitas, California, December 22, 1969).

. . . it is no longer possible to build homes that most Americans can rent or buy without massive subsidy. Even HUD's Operation Breakthrough, a crash pro-

1. California Migrant Master Plan: Progress Report, 1966 (State Office of Economic Opportunity, Sacramento, Calif.).

gram to industrialize housing production, will affect quantities more than costs. (Ada Louise Huxtable, *New York Times*, reported in *San Jose Mercury-News*, November 9, 1969. Copyright 1969 by *The New York Times Company*. Reprinted by permission.

The solution to housing needs for Mexican-Americans will come only when this need for all American poor is met satisfactorily.

chapter **6**

# The Political Scene

Sharing in the full life in America is inexorably linked with the scheme of politics. A voice and a force that command attention and action are requisites for this. For a variety of reasons, perhaps, Mexican-Americans of the Southwest are not a vital part of these politics.

Whatever the definition, politics is a base for action and achieving ends. To be excluded or to withdraw from this engagement means living by decisions of others. In America's system of representative government, the numerous political groups are constantly maneuvering for control, or at least for an influence in the use of this power. Mexican-Americans are not part of this drama. Except for a few geopolitical areas such as New Mexico, they have never really been a serious part of the system except as commodities manipulated for the advantage of others.

If visions are to go beyond mere talk, Mexican-Americans must awaken to the reality that short of total revolution and collapse of the system, which does not seem imminent, the burden of entering the political arena rests on their shoulders. No complete alternative is apparent. Aloofness from action means acquiescence to political decisions and implementation by others.

The burning question today for MAPA (Mexican-American Political Association), for example, is how to be politically influential.[1] A number of obvious strategies are possible. Individuals or groups may affiliate with the major political parties and attempt to bring change from within for partisan as well as group and personal gains. Extremists now and then trumpet a goal of creating separate political parties. In other words, a separatist movement or a third party is advocated. It appears that except for isolated political units in the Southwest this strategy has little hope of acceptance. Too few, if any, political units exist in which Mexican-Americans are concentrated in large

---

1. MAPA's militant political views are illustrated in their Issues Conference resolutions shown in Appendix A.

enough numbers to constitute the majority of the potential or the registered voters.

Politics has, at the best, indirectly benefited Mexican-Americans. Young militants are discovering reality to be the exclusion, or non-involvement, of members of the ethnic group in active politics. When involved in political campaigns, they perform almost exclusively as the "troops" but never as the "colonels" or "generals." Elected offices and appointments of any consequence always go to someone else.

Considering the size of Spanish-surnamed populations, New Mexico has achieved proportionately greater political vitality when compared to any of the five Southwestern states.[2] California is perhaps the least productive of these states though it has the greatest Spanish-surname population. Historical antecedents of New Mexico and the isolative factors that have kept communities intact are a partial explanation for that state. The rural character of New Mexico and this isolation of communities and counties have enabled bloc voting.[3]

Several observations may be made about cities with large Mexican-descent populations. For example, political gains and offices in El Paso, Texas, have been dominated by Anglo-Americans. The substantial numbers of middle-class Latins (Mexican-Americans) living there have been politically inert. A number of reasons are suggested by observers for the weakness of the total political situation. Mexican-Americans in El Paso (1) are poor, (2) are poorly educated, (3) persist in retaining their Mexican rather than Anglo-American cultural ways, (4) distrust government and politicians, (5) remain relatively content with the status quo, and (6) face discrimination from Anglo-Americans. Consequently, political candidates feel they get limited returns; so they do not invest much time wooing Mexicans who will not vote.[4]

Mexican-American organizations such as LULAC (League of United Latin American Citizens) and PASSO (Political Association of Spanish-speaking Organizations) have in the last few years initiated energetic campaigns to arouse the flagging political spirit of the people. At the same time, recently activated militants declare these organizations too middle-class and out of touch with the problems of the grass-roots communities. These militants frequently refuse to support or covertly sabotage the political efforts of the older units. Success has been irregular; heretofore the substantial num-

2. The Honorable Joseph Montoya of New Mexico is the *one* Mexican-American senator in the United States.
3. Horacio Ulbarri, "Educational Needs of the Mexican-American," National Conference on Educational Opportunities for Mexican-Americans (Austin, Texas, April 25–26, 1968), p. 8.
4. Edward C. Banfield, *Big City Politics* (New York: Random House, Inc., 1965), pp. 66–79, 80–93.

ber of middle-class Mexicans have not readily supported these organizational drives. Undoubtedly this social class will have to be thoroughly involved if any great change is to take place.

The city of Los Angeles, California, contains a similar political vacuum. The one congressman of Mexican descent, Edward C. Roybal, and its one state legislator, Alex Garcia, are the only elected political figures to federal and state political offices. Recently, with an unprecedented support from other groups, Julian Nava won a seat on the Los Angeles City Board of Education. These gains are not inconsequential, but they represent only a fraction of the representation needed.

In San Francisco, attorney Robert Gonzales received an appointment to the board of supervisors and Dr. David J. Sanchez, Jr., to the board of education. Throughout the state of California irregular gains are made in elections to various governing boards. This is promising, but it is premature to consider this a trend. Substantial gains will have to come before Mexican-Americans can claim any significant ability to influence political and civic matters.

Friends have bluntly stated that unless Mexican-Americans become actively involved in political action they will continue as a marginal group. Accepting the truism that a group *wins* power rather than having it bestowed, Mexican-Americans in northern California recently campaigned for a major public office. An account follows of the 25th Assembly District, California Democratic primary elections of 1968.

This political district has a large, but not a majority, Spanish-surname population. Democrats are a majority in registration, but a Republican legislator is the incumbent. The campaign waged, though not successful in its primary objective, laid to rest a good many myths and bared a few uncomfortable truths about political pragmatism.

For the political race, community leadership screened and selected a candidate. Considerable care was exerted because tales, true and fictional, of communities fragmented by too many ethnic candidates all running for the same office were uppermost in the minds of the organizers.[5] This care was exerted even though everyone was aware that neither major political party is monolithic and that at no one time does it truly represent all its constituency on all issues.

The nomination of a Mexican-American by the community organizations created consternation within the ranks of the county Democratic committee. Two sore spots were apparent: County Democrats were not invited

5. Divide and conquer is the tried and tested tactic against political interlopers, and groups in power may be expected to encourage discord.

to participate in the selection of the candidate, and more important, they had made an earlier commitment to a candidate of their choosing.

Support came immediately to the Chicano campaign from the Mexican-American community. This contribution was substantial and disputes the constant allegation from the majority group (and to some extent within the ethnic group itself) that Mexican-American communities do not support their candidates. To be sure, not all individuals were financial contributors, but many were indirect supporters. One group of veterans, for example, organized and implemented the total political poster phase of the campaign.

In the course of the campaign, support came from a variety of Anglos, Mexican-Americans, other minorities, Democrats, and some Republicans. Immediately, too, opposition or failure to support came from at least some members of all of these groups. To place this in a proper perspective, it is important to note that this phenomenon is found in every political effort. The constant admonition of critics that Mexican-Americans must insure total backing before entry into a race is a condition too frequently applied to minorities to discourage them from political candidacy but not expected of majority group candidates.

In the course of the political race, encouragement came from many unexpected sources. This is a good omen for future political plans. And at the same time, it is important to identify those major factors that militated against winning this particular political race.

Democratic party leaders of the area, in spite of their public postures, were not ready nor willing to give support to the Mexican-American community. As a result, traditional sources of political finances from party-backers and others did not materialize. Sympathizers, for whatever reason, did contribute funds and personal services, of course, but the major blocks of party volunteers and monies normally encouraged were directed elsewhere. The decision of the party to support elsewhere made it impossible to recruit prominent Anglo personalities for key positions in the visible campaign organization. Some liberals did serve in advisory capacities.

Practically all Mexican-Americans in the political campaign were experienced, having to their credit many hours and campaigns in behalf of party candidates. They were thoroughly familiar with get-out-the-vote operations and strategies for successful campaign planning.[6] Needed were much practical support and less theoretical orientations, and certainly the former did not happen.

---

6. Examples of well-studied sources are D. Swing Meyer, *The Winning Candidate* (New York: James H. Heineman, Inc., 1966) and *Voting Is People Power* (League of Women Voters Education Fund, 1200 Seventeenth Street, N.W., Washington, D.C. 20036. April 1967).

The fourth major factor that shook the campaign effort was the national political campaigns of Hubert H. Humphrey, Robert J. Kennedy, and Eugene McCarthy, each of whom needed visible Mexican-American support in California. These personalities were successful in enticing some of the experienced and politically oriented individuals from the local effort.

In spite of all these circumstances, the political effort was not a complete loss. Some supporters considered the effort quite respectable in accomplishment. Others sensed a betrayal of the Democratic party regulars and refused to support party efforts in the general elections; as a consequence the incumbent retained his seat.

These highlights of the campaign were exhilarating: an unprecedented response from heretofore reportedly lackadaisical Mexican-American voters; a number of Anglo liberals served *la causa* unselfishly; the weekly newspaper of the area endorsed and editorialized sympathetically; individuals other than Mexican-Americans offered facilities and services; veterans from the ethnic group and other adults organized and carried out crucial assignments; college students brought with them a refreshing zest; and, of course, a new political and community leadership emerged.

Believing politics to be crucial, Mexican-Americans organized political leadership conferences in the sixties throughout the Southwest. A number of basic orientations are products of these interactions between national political thinkers and membership of the ethnic groups.

The basic guideline for this cadre of activists has become *think politically*. Mexican-Americans must recognize that policy is made by the political and economic power structure and that policy is for and in the interests of the establishment; Chicanos must therefore learn to identify the levels of power in the local, state, and federal systems. Typically, the power to control money and political appointments is dominated by the Anglo-American political parties. To become decisive factors in politics, Mexican-Americans must build this kind of power.

In order to move toward this power, they must tap their sources of strength such as concentrations of ethnic voter populations, ethnic membership in the trade union movement, ethnic organizations which are stable and efficient and coalitions with political, age, ethnic, economic, and social minorities.

One important idea yet to receive full attention is the indispensable need to focus on critical universal issues, which will also lead to permanent gains for Mexican-Americans, rather than on exclusively ethnic-oriented protests and tactics.

The future of Mexican-American political efforts can only be conjectural at this moment. It appears reasonable to predict, however, that it will not be an easy matter to win strong party support in this community or throughout the Southwest for Mexican-American candidates. One thing seems certain, Mexican-Americans must develop political sophistication and positions of leverage as they continue aggressive involvement in *both* major political parties if changes are to be concrete. Fundamentally, Mexican-Americans need to remember always that legislative enactment is influenced by political muscle; in addition, they must remember that the control of political power is zealously guarded and is not given away freely.

# chapter 7

# Chicano Voices

Mexican-Americans of the sixties reflect the mood of American minorities which demands self-determination. Conferences and seminars about Mexican-American affairs over the last several decades typically have been dominated by others than Mexican-Americans. While legitimate reasons exist for continued concern by all on the topic of Chicano problems, the trend today is toward an unprecedented role by Mexican-Americans in planning and implementation of conferences.

With this orientation in mind, the discussion that follows reflects views coming directly from Mexican-Americans. These voices are unrelenting in their insistence that the social scene needs major reform.

To understand the status of the Mexican-Americans in America, basic questions must be asked first. What is the Mexican culture which Mexican-Americans are said to retain? What is the Anglo-American culture orientation necessary for participation and sharing in the goods and services today? Who and what is the Mexican-American in the United States today? Is there a unique Mexican-American culture? What regional differences, if any, are to be noted in individuals from El Paso, Albuquerque, Los Angeles, Tucson, San Jose; urban or rural; first generation or tenth generation, educated or illiterate; poor or affluent; militant, moderate, conservative; articulate or silent? Current observations and contemporary studies, though limited in number, clearly indicate Americans of Mexican descent are indeed diverse.

Notwithstanding these variants, many problems facing Mexican-Americans are real and demand solutions. The visible problems and the socio-economic subordination of the group are the symbols to which most activists respond. It is this point of view that is articulated, often emotionally, in the conferences held throughout the nation. It is to this that militants and activists are geared for action. But current activities can be understood best with an historical perspective.

The historical marches into the Southwest by Juan de Oñate and subsequent Spanish explorers, the founding of scattered towns throughout the Southwest, the saga of an Hispanic-oriented way of life, social, economic, and political, are described in a number of publications.[1] The literature readily available to the general reading public tends to contain standardized accounts. Most materials found in schools are from an Anglophilic point of view. Generally, the coverage in history textbooks is limited to a few highlights of Hispanic adventure. And that is all. Some scholars, obviously, have studied painstakingly this historic period in depth, but most readers are not scholars, and few publications of consequence are available for general reading.

Who are the Mexican-Americans today? The Inter-Agency Committee on Mexican American Affairs describes them as follows:

> The Mexican American may be a descendant of the Spanish explorers Cortez, Cabeza de Baca [sic] or Coronado. Or he may have recently immigrated from Mexico and may very well be a descendant of the great Aztec civilization. Or he may be a mestizo from the union of Indian and Spanish. . . .

> As the Anglo American moved out into the frontier lands of our Nation, the Mexican American gave way as did the American Indian. He lost lands which he had held for centuries; he lost his footings in his own community. He became the governed in his village. His language, which had been the tongue of commerce, became a mark of the "foreigner." Suddenly this was no longer his land or home.

> The Mexican Americans were pushed into menial jobs as the years passed; their children rarely reaped the benefits of education. There appeared in towns, villages and cities certain poor sections, or barrios—the ghettos of Mexican Americans. Caught in a vicious circle, the Mexican Americans set the patterns of poverty which their children, to the present, encounter.

> There are approximately 10 million Spanish-surnamed citizens in our country, of which six and a half million reside in the Southwest. In 1960, Mexican Americans represented over 12 percent of the total population in the five Southwestern States; this group is the largest minority in each of these States.[2]

There can be little argument with the broad strokes of this picture. What is not adequately suggested, much less discussed, are the growing sources of untapped talent and achievement of educated Mexican-Americans found in every major community.

The plight of the many poor is painful and it is to this the many articulate spokesmen address themselves. An activist at the Southwest Council of

1. Odie B. Faulk, *Land of Many Frontiers: A History of the American Southwest* (New York: Oxford University Press, 1968). [And others.]
2. *The Mexican American: A New Focus on Opportunity* (Inter-Agency Committee on Mexican American Affairs, 1800 G. Street, N.W., Washington, D.C., 1967–1968).

La Raza scored the existing economic and social gap between the Mexican-Americans in the Southwest and the rest of the nation.[3]

He recommended that funds and technical cooperation be made available to Mexican-American organizations and individuals who already had amply demonstrated their innate talents and capabilities for solving this problem.

Responding to the appeals of Mexican-Americans, a national foundation made funds available to the Southwest Council of La Raza to implement its efforts in creating a mechanism for establishing priorities of Mexican-American needs and creating a machinery to attack these needs.[4]

Much has been said about Mexican ethnic culture values and their relationship to the status of the group. While this culture has strengths in its original setting, when transported to the Southwest culture insufficiencies have been noted in its clash with dominant American orientations. If these ethnic culture values are worth retaining, how are they to mesh or survive without conflict in America today?

It has been suggested that areas of conflict today, for example, lie in (1) the lack of competition, (2) the timidity, (3) the present-time orientation, and (4) the low levels of aspiration so frequently referred to among Mexican-Americans, who also tend to be poor. It is important to note that when the social class is held constant, the matter of *time orientation* for Mexican-Americans, for example, is not really different from the rest of the society. The key point in this analysis of ethnic characteristics is "that the majority of the Mexican-Americans are found in the ranks of the poor and the uneducated."[5] Following are additional data:

In the five Southwestern states, Mexican Americans, 14 years of age and older, have only 8.1 years of schooling, compared with 12.0 years for the average Anglo-American of the same age.

Mexican American children have a school drop-out rate of 8 to 13 percent in 1966 as compared to a national average of 4 percent for that year.

Mexican Americans in barrios had an unemployment rate of 8 to 13 percent in 1966 as compared to a national average of 4 percent for that year.

Subemployment rates for Spanish-surnamed residents of the slums were 42 to 47 percent.

Employment of Mexican Americans by the Federal Government was in need of attention. The Civil Service Commission report indicated, for example, that the Selective Service Board had no Spanish-surnamed employees above the Grade of

3. Ernesto Galarza, in *Southwest Council of La Raza* (First Annual Report, March 1969), pp. 2, 7, 8.
4. Ibid.
5. Horacio Ulibarri, "Educational Needs of the Mexican American," National Conference on Educational Opportunities for Mexican-Americans (Austin, Texas, April 25–26, 1968).

GS-8, and in the Department of Justice, only 62 top-level positions out of a total of 11,695 were held by Mexican Americans.

The 1959 family income under $3,000 of urban Spanish-surnamed families was 28.5 percent in Arizona; 17.5 percent in California; 28.6 percent in Colorado; 33.1 percent in New Mexico; and 47.3 percent in Texas.

The 1959 family income under $3,000 of rural Spanish surnamed families was 50.4 percent in Colorado; 53.8 percent in New Mexico; and 69.2 percent in Texas.[6]

Other problems chronically facing young Mexican-Americans in their effort to succeed in America's schools are reported as (1) a family environment not oriented to success in schools, (2) a school system which is confusing and alien, (3) guidance personnel who fail to understand and support Mexican-Americans, (4) the lack of scholarships and grants, and (5) the nonexistence of continuity of philanthropic foundation aid for Mexican-Americans.

Inadequacies in both Spanish and English are frequent deficiencies noted in Mexican-American youth. Some are caught between the clash of cultures: Mexican and Anglo, the school and the home, and "the maladjustments of the Anglo world of materialism and technology and the Hispanic world of humanism and emotional temperament."[7]

Because the grave needs of the poor Mexican-American individuals and families must be considered, sight is often lost of the diversity within the group. Needs are real; the diversity is real. But the needs of one segment are not the needs of the other. Sensitivity and selectivity in recommending an order of priorities are necessary.

Studying Mexican-Americans a researcher found them scattered over the occupational range. They were educated scholars and professionals as well as illiterate and unskilled laborers. Though this situation is found in many other groups as well, Mexican-Americans were overrepresented in the lower levels of educational achievement and occupations.[8]

Still another writer commented that though they are found today in positions of prestige and status and more youth are finishing high schools and entering colleges, educators and other public officials must not become complacent. *Too many students continue to fail and drop out of our schools.*[9]

6. Ibid.
7. Manuel H. Guerra, "The Retention of Mexican American Students in Higher Education with Special Reference to Bicultural and Bilingual Problems" (Conference, California State College, Long Beach, May 15–17, 1969), pp. 17, 5, 4, 16, 11.
8. Horacio Ulibarri, "Educational Needs of the Mexican American."
9. Marguerite Smith, "English as a Second Language for Mexican Americans," National Conference on Educational Opportunities for Mexican-Americans (Austin, Texas, April 25–26, 1968), pp. 1, 5.

It is well to note that the determination of youth and their families to succeed in school is high. They need support.[10]

A Mexican-American cannot be stereotyped. He is "not one person, he is many peoples, he is many persons, culturally and in every conceivable way."[11] Because of this variation "generalizations about the Spanish-Mexican or the Mexican-American are always wrong."[12] It is clear no monolithic group exists that is Mexican-American. It is diverse just as so many others.

Notwithstanding current visible gains of individuals, the image of Mexican-Americans as it appears in the current literature, the public media, and public opinion is not highly favorable. Militant students in high schools, colleges, and universities express their discontent with this image of the Mexican-American, and they are quick to charge the educational system with gross neglect, if not criminal culpability. These students particularly recognize the cruciality of higher education for economic and social success in American society. The efforts of militant students, therefore, are to open channels of entry and achievement in colleges and universities.

Charges that American higher education fails Mexican-Americans are many. In California, for example, every campus has a chapter of UMAS (United Mexican-American Students), MASC (Mexican-American Student Confederation), MAYO (Mexican-American Youth Organization), MECHA (Mŏvimiento Estudiantil Chicano de Aztlán) or similar organizations. And they are all militant groups expressing deep convictions and a need for reform. Most public or private colleges and universities with large Mexican-American populations have been challenged aggressively by Chicanos. Available statistics indicate that higher education can only show extremely limited enrollments and graduations of Mexican-Americans. Supporting programs which subsidize or provide scholarship grants and living costs are today extremely scarce.[13] The future of these programs is uncertain.

Students at the University of California at Los Angeles may serve to illustrate the current student mobilization against higher education inertia. Students disclose that the Mexican-American enrollment at UCLA is no more than two percent of 26,000 full-time students, and Chicano graduate students are only 1.3 percent of the total graduate enrollment. Other criticisms include the lack of Mexican-American studies and credentials. Student militants accuse the university of neglect. They maintain that anything of

10. Philip Montez, "Mexicanismo vs. Retention" (Conference, California State College, Long Beach, May 15–17, 1969), pp. 4, 15.

11. George I. Sanchez, in *"Mexican-American Seminar,"* mimeographed (Phoenix, Arizona, January 18, 1963), pp. 7, 9.

12. Ibid.

13. While official data are not available, an observation of colleges and universities suggests that a *smaller proportion* of total educational opportunity program funds are diverted to Chicano students.

importance for the Chicano student community has through necessity been initiated and conducted by Chicanos themselves. The alienation of these students from the institution is apparent.[14] At the same time, this detachment is the more poignant because higher education, for these students, holds the key to self-determination in professions, economics, politics, and personal life. This conclusion is inescapable.

Academic debate over the meaning of traditional college standards is more than a deliberation for Mexican-Americans. Conventional criteria are a concrete barrier placed in the way of education. If today's children of the affluent middle-class Anglo family find irrelevancy in current curriculums and standards, the reaction from articulate Mexican-Americans fighting this issue is understandable.

Much has been said about the middle-class Anglo-American orientation in the typical college admission requirements and curriculum content. The many essays, monographs, articles, and books clearly consider this orientation a disservice to *all* American disadvantaged and alienated. In addition to that already expressed about the socially disadvantaged, the Mexican-American hard-core poor show at least two other facets. Mexican-Americans are descendants of a Mexican culture. This is a mestizo culture composed essentially of the Spanish and the Indian cultures found in middle Mexico. This culture and the Spanish language are two principal variables not found in the analysis of differences in other American subgroups.

Quite understandably, then, the young militants in confronting the colleges and universities are demanding a reform in admission standards, a relevant definition of academic performance, and a thorough curriculum overhaul.[15] Chicano youth join other students in accusing the entire educational system as one geared to *screen people out* of the learning process rather than responding to the challenge of education for all.[16]

Some disillusionment of activists with the role of the educational system and process lies in the Chicanos' growing awareness and sensitivity to their own backgrounds. In fighting for a chance to succeed in college, the Mexican-Americans are also combating stresses and strains from the home. Some attend colleges and universities without parental support, and their presence is evidence of a rebellion rather than familial conformity. This is a classic example of generational and culture conflict.

14. United Mexican American Students, "Retention of the Chicano Student as a Comprehensive Program Unit of the Mexican American Student Organization" (Conference, California State College, Long Beach, May 15–17, 1969), pp. 5, 8, 14–18.
15. *Proceedings of the Conference on Increasing Opportunities for Mexican American Students in Higher Education* (California State College, Long Beach, May 15–17, 1969), p. 42.
16. Guerra, pp. 17, 5, 4, 16, 11.

Curriculum relevance has been a topic for philosophic debate for a long time; it is now a call for active confrontation. Youth who speak out belittle current curricular practices, and Mexican-Americans are included in this group. Many ideas are propounded for improvement of education for Mexican-Americans. Overgeneralizing and stereotyping, however, must be avoided if the maximum number are to be well served by change.[17]

There is no doubt that the appropriateness of today's curriculums for all must be reexamined. In so doing, and while acknowledging the full richness of the Mexican cultural heritage, educational programs must enable these Mexican-American youth to achieve those rewards that serve as a spur for society in general. Inevitably this means mobility for individuals and modifications of culture patterns.[18]

It also appears clear the individual must be free to select from many choices. Any restriction of alternatives must be considered prejudicial to the person. He must be free of all extraneous restrictions in this matter.

Prejudicial attitudes and discrimination are encountered by many Mexican-American students. Major studies in the nation indict America for its prejudices and discriminatory practices toward ethnic and racial minorities. Clearly, negative attitudes are a broad societal problem, and improvement in majority America is desired, of course. But it is well to remember that everyone has biases and prejudices—Anglos toward Mexican-Americans and Mexican-Americans toward Anglos. Change becomes a two-way street, and genuine efforts to bridge these gaps must be made by all. Inevitably, marked and conspicuous perpetuation of hostile relationships becomes counterproductive. Humans tend to retreat in defense, if in a subordinate role, and to reinforce the very points of contrast and friction. This makes recovery of ground that much more difficult.[19]

The self-image of Mexican-Americans may be but a mirroring of the perceived Anglo-American view of Mexicans. Reports are rather consistent in citing inferiority feelings of Mexican-Americans.[20] Public opinion and writers frequently mention the low motivation in Mexican-Americans as an explanation for failure to succeed in schools. The school and community are blamed for the internalization by the pupil of feelings of futility, frustration,

---

17. Herbert B. Wilson, "Evaluation of the Influence of Educational Programs on Mexican-Americans" (Conference, California State College, Long Beach, May 15–17, 1969), pp. 21, 22.
18. Ibid.
19. Frank Angel, "Program Content to Meet the Educational Needs of Mexican-Amercans," National Conference on Educational Opportunities for Mexican-Americans (Austin, Texas, April 25–26, 1968), pp. 4, 5, 7.
20. Mexican-American Study Project, Progress Report No. 9, University of California, Los Angeles, May 1967.

and self-doubt.[21] Wherever the blame lies for feelings of inadequacies, Mexican-Americans make it quite clear that they believe schools are gross contributors to the problem.

Teachers are the key to any good educational program. Quality education for all requires teachers not only professionally trained but also understanding and empathic. Mexican-American students have known many excellent Anglo-American teachers. But good teachers of Mexican-American descent are also needed in great numbers. Any curriculum reform requiring a firsthand knowledge of the culture and an ability to speak Spanish will require large numbers of Mexican-Americans entering the teaching field. Few administrators argue the need today, but recruitment efforts, genuine or perfunctory, usually result in few teachers recruited in any but the choicest districts. Unfortunately, experienced teachers are often displaced from one district where they are badly needed to another which offers more of those things attractive to teachers in general. The recruitment of Mexican-American teachers today is a matter of robbing Peter to pay Paul.

A reality to be faced throughout the entire Southwest is that credentialed teachers of Mexican or Spanish-speaking descent are in very short supply. What else can be expected with so few numbers of Mexican-Americans attending colleges and universities over the recent decades? Further, not all Mexican-Americans who attend colleges go into teaching as a profession—nor should they. Some are not suited for teaching; others are personally motivated toward other occupations such as medicine, dentistry, law, social services, business, and many other professions important to the upward movement of the individual and the group.

Consequently, any program based on an assumption that a ready supply of Spanish-speaking teachers is available for educational programs is in serious difficulty before it begins. Another disconcerting fact has to do with the appropriateness and quality of varying levels of language competency. For numerous reasons many Mexican-Americans have forgotten or never acquired Spanish-language skills. Few who speak it with facility are competently trained in linguistics or teaching aspects. While the promise of bilingual-oriented programs is most engaging, it should be clear to proponents that scarcity of essential resources poses a serious problem.[22]

A bitter pill though it may be to swallow, the foregoing seems to be an honest assessment of supply and demand of Mexican-American teachers. The censure of militants accusing the educational system of fraud and loss

21. Julian Samora, in "Mexican-American Seminar," mimeographed (Phoenix, Arizona, January 18, 1963), p. 11.
22. Frank Angel, pp. 4, 5, 7.

of both culture and language can be better understood. Regrettably, too many accounts are true that in both secondary schools as well as colleges and universities the first to fail in Spanish language programs are students of Spanish-speaking ancestry.

In the future of America, the majority of occupational choices will continue to require more than high school graduation. The community college with its broad philosophic orientation contains a tremendous potential of service for Mexican-Americans.[23] The open-door policy of educational services to the community is indeed a promise; unfortunately, it has tended to be a "revolving door" for many Mexican-Americans. The community college, along with other educational organizations, needs substantial reform before it can do justice to the promise it offers all its students. All that is said about curriculum reform, standards of achievement, flexibility within the programs, and nurture of a sense of identity and achievement are needed change. The community college has the *greatest* potential for contribution to the adult aspirations of the Mexican-American population. With proper restructure, its transfer, terminal, and cultural programs can achieve more easily what a four-year college or university cannot. Mexican-American activists and schools should strive to increase this enrollment. An unfortunate tendency exists which pushes academically weak students in educational opportunity programs directly into four-year colleges. These colleges unfortunately are less equipped to do the job than are community colleges.

Before some community colleges can serve their students optimally, however, they must get rid of the notion that they are traditional junior universities. Too frequently all courses in the junior college are no different than those in a four-year institution, and when this happens there is really no choice between community or four-year colleges.[24]

Students charge teachers and schools with prejudice. Mexican-Americans are spoken of as "beaners, greasers, taco-benders, and wetbacks." The Mexicans are stereotyped as undesirables, and an identity conflict is created for students and self-hate is intensified.[25] Schools and teachers are to be found where this description does not apply. Important, however, is that too many schools are accused of this, and militants are charging wide-scale inferior practices. Positive programs will be needed before these students gain confidence. If the community colleges make no appreciable reform, then a golden opportunity is lost.

23. Refer to James W. Thornton, Jr., *The Community Junior College*, 2nd ed. (New York: John Wiley and Sons, Inc., 1966).
24. Chicano Ethnic Studies Class, "Problems of Retention as Seen by Mexican American Students" (Conference, California State College, Long Beach, May 15–17, 1969), pp. 1, 6.
25. *Proceedings of the National Conference on Educational Opportunities for Mexican Americans* (Austin, Texas, April 25–26, 1968), pp. 25, 27.

Demands for change and improvement in educational programs come from many groups. Mexican-American community militants want instant initiation of ethnic s†udy programs. It is interesting, and a little sad, to note that most of the suggestions now made were heard years ago. In the past they were couched in the diplomatic language of the profession; the big difference today is that demands are stated in unrelenting and abrasive language. It would appear that those in charge and responsible for curriculum suitability are reaping results of neglect, rigidity, tradition-mindedness, and of insensitivity. Student demands for change are indeed a confrontation.

Articulate and angry Chicano college and university students have formulated resolutions and demands intended to erase ineffective practices and to hurry the initiation of new ones.[26] Recommendations focus on the need for Mexican-American or Chicano Ethnic Studies at both undergraduate as well as graduate levels, educational financial assistance programs of different kinds, and talent-search programs to increase the number of potentially able Mexican-Americans in higher education. Further suggestions include tutoring programs; remedial courses in the basics of English, mathematics, and reading; assistance in housing problems for students; and greatly increased and improved guidance services throughout the spectrum of students' needs. Changes are slow in implementation, and it seems reasonable to expect continued agitation and insistence for these changes to occur.

26. Anna Nieto Gomez and J. Anthony Vasquez, "The Needs of the Chicano on the College Campus" (Conference, California State College, Long Beach, May 15–17, 1969); Monte E. Perez, Maria Diaz, and Oscar Martinez, "Retention of Mexican American Students in College" (Conference, California State College, Long Beach, May 15–17, 1969), pp. 3, 4; United Mexican American Students, pp. 5, 8, 14–18.

# chapter 8

# The New Religion

Expressing frustration and disenchantment with established institutions is a phenomenon peculiar also to Chicanos. The Catholic Church, long considered a holdout against the liberalization of its traditional role in a changing world, is under attack by Mexican-Americans. Clearly, this militancy is not an isolated instance of rebellion against the religious establishment. It reflects the mood of activist Chicanos as well as the generalized discontent throughout the nation.

Liberals fight for reform within the Church.[1] Reform is a necessary condition for its survival as an integral institution in the lives of many. But all present signs suggest that any restructure will result only from aggressive confrontation against the vested authorities. The Catholic Church is not alone in facing this assault. All major religious denominations may expect or are experiencing this challenge.

Growing numbers of Mexican-Americans perceive the Catholic Church differently today than formerly. This observation may not be true, of course, of an older and more conservative generation still responding to conditioned patterns of behavior inculcated by doctrinal teachings.

Frenetically searching for self, militant youth explore historical accounts of Mexico and the American Southwest. They are rediscovering accounts of the conquest of Mexico and of the exploration and colonization of its northern territories. The role and significance of the Church now takes on new dimensions, as do the religious individuals accompanying the adventurers. These priests and monks were unquestionably men possessed of courage, endurance, and purpose. It took these kinds of people to establish the flag, the sword, and the cross in New Spain. Today, militant Mexican-

---

1. The Catholic Church in Mexico itself looks to change and recommended the use of its influence for the liberal solution of human problems. The historical conservative position of the Church makes this posture profoundly significant (*San Jose News*, May 17, 1965).

Americans are learning that these same men, in the name of the Church, organized, developed, and exploited the subjugated people. Possibly all these and more were products of a time of history, but many young Chicanos are becoming aware for the first time, and this tends to aggravate misgivings toward the Church.

Second- and third-generation Mexican-Americans, in many cases, recall homespun tales about the "old days of Mexico." In some instances, anti-clerical views at one time heatedly pronounced by some in Mexico are retold, and added to these are tales, true or otherwise, of exploitation of the common people by the Church and the wealthy. This seems a conspiracy. An account of the historical image of the Catholic Church in Mexico follows:

> Throughout its history, the Catholic Church in Mexico has been the instrument of reaction, according to most Mexican historians. They cite the facts that the church opposed the war for independence, sparked the war of the reform, and sponsored the attempts to place Maximilian on the throne.
>
> The clergy also fought the revolution of 1910, condemned the constitution of 1917 and started the Cristeros uprising a decade later in which militant Catholics burned government schools, dynamited a train and started a full-scale civil war in which thousands were killed. (Ruben Salazar, the *Los Angeles Times*, reported in the *San Jose News*, May 17, 1968. Copyright, 1968, *Los Angeles Times*. Reprinted by permission.)

This growing disenchantment with the Church as an institution is exacerbated by documented history. From the beginning in Mexico the religious leadership of the Church was European not Mexican. Foreigners dominated. In the Southwest, especially after the territorial acquisition by the United States following the Mexican War of 1846–1848, the Spanish-speaking clergy were gradually but ruthlessly displaced. Replacing the Hispano priests were the Irish. These Irish priests were total foreigners to the culture of the Southwest and its religious traditions, and believing their "Church" superior, they made vigorous efforts to stamp out the "decadent" Catholic practices found there. In terse words, Hispanos, their clergy, and church practices were inferior and were to be cleaned up. This undoubtedly promoted defection by Hispanos.

The Catholic hierarchy of America excluded Mexican-descent and Hispano priests and substituted them almost exclusively with upwardly mobile Irish priests. This institutionalized racism is a conspicuous part of the total fabric of today's Catholic Church which Mexican-American militants and liberals resent. (A review of names of the prominent religious leaders of the Church today establishes the relevance of this view.)

These views color the emotions of the militants and further predispose them to changing views and attitudes toward the Catholic Church. The recent bold challenge of militants is reinforced by the publicly aired position of liberal Protestants and Jews who are insistent that religious institutions be involved. At the same time the visibility of ministers and rabbis in protest marches are equated with white America's involvement in the human rights struggle. To be sure, priests, nuns, and seminarians are participating in these protests in growing numbers, but militants see these individuals as rebelling also against the rigidity of an hierarchical Church system.

Militants assert that the Church, to which an estimated 70 to 90 percent of the Mexican-Americans belong, has abandoned the ethnic group. Major problems needing attention are the day-to-day needs of the poor, such as employment, housing, hunger, education, and health. An invidious comparison is made with other religious groups. Stated rather bluntly is the assertion that the Church is chiefly responsible for the stoic and self-effacing postures of Mexican-descent people and that the Church as a highly centralized structure is most concerned with material self-aggrandizement. These latter qualities attributed to the Church are challenged as irrelevant to the present-day needs of Mexican-Americans.

Activists find support for their disaffection in the public questioning of the role of religion. Theological students and seminarians over the nation are raising grave questions about the proper role of the churches in today's world of conflict. Repeatedly, dissidents from the traditional programs of religious life preparation rebel against the failure of the Church to respond to the morality of the American war in Southeast Asia. The Church organizational structure is considered overly centralized in administration and insensitive to variations in local and regional needs. Religious trainees appear to reflect a need for local control, but not under the old-line authoritarian administrators. These administrators must be replaced to make the Church relevant today.

Generally, theological students and seminarians hold little faith in self-renewal from within the institutions. Rather, they believe that change will come as a result of a more radical approach.

Major clashes are further illustrations of the discontent with the inaction of religious bodies. In East Harlem a youth group, protesting church officials' refusal to permit facilities for a free-lunch program, barricaded itself inside the First Spanish Methodist Church. Court action was used to eject the demonstrators.

In another instance, a Catholic priest was dismissed from his teaching position in which he argued the relevance of involvement in social problems by the religious person. Obviously, the hierarchy did not agree with this view.[2]

2. This dispute was submitted to a committee of priests which ruled the suspended priest be allowed to return to his teaching. This procedure is a break with tradition (*San Jose Mercury*, January 10, 1970).

Traditional deference to a pastor was ignored by angry Mexican-Americans and supporters in East Los Angeles. A reported 300 demonstrators from the organization "Católicos Por la Raza" and its supporters protested during a midnight Christmas mass. Mexican-Americans were objecting to a three million dollar church building rather than the investment in the poverty, education, and low-cost housing needs of the people. Five Mexican-American demonstrators were arrested. Militants charged the Church with hypocrisy.[3]

Catholic religious people are caught in a dilemma. On the one hand, they sense an urgency for involvement in their communities, and on the other a feeling of responsibility to the Church. A clear solution at this moment seems remote. These priests, nuns, and seminarians find themselves in deep personal conflict. They are compelled to respond to the human forces within their parishes. Failure to do so means alienation and ineffectiveness. If they support legitimate community protests against dehumanizing situations, they run the risk of subjecting themselves to the censure of the Church hierarchy which disapproves of rocking the status quo. Regardless of the conflict, many priests, nuns, and seminarians have chosen involvement as a primary moral commitment in a contemporary society while at the same time they continue to plead for understanding and support from the Church establishment.

Recently, impelled by the rising social tensions and in response to an invitation by the Chicano Priests Organization of Santa Clara County (California), priests, sisters, and laymen from California, Oregon, and Washington held a meeting in Los Gatos, California, and organized the "West Coast Coalition of Priests and Sisters Working with the Spanish-speaking."

The new Coalition passed resolutions in support of the Spanish-speaking in their struggle for better jobs and housing, equal treatment and justice under the law.[4] The priests and sisters believe that an urgent priority of the Church is to become actively involved in solving the social problems facing the Spanish-speaking. This action on the part of these religious persons carries vital implications for a precedent within the Church as well as the manner of working with a community.

A growing number of priests are marching shoulder-to-shoulder with Mexican-Americans in protesting lack of jobs and housing. These religious people are arrested with other protesters.[5] Catholic nuns steadfastly insist they must play their role in a contemporary society—a role impossible to carry out behind cloistered walls. Catholic chaplains at colleges and univer-

---

3. *San Jose Mercury*, January 5, 1970.
4. The complete resolutions are shown with permission of the West Coalition of Priests and Sisters in Appendix B.
5. *Sun*, San Jose, California, December 17, 1969.

sities walk a tight line between students' idealistic dissent and the conservative traditions of the Church. Many priests make the choice to support student protests.

Catholic universities are beginning to provide increased opportunities to minorities and among whom are included Mexican-Americans. At this moment, however, they perform no better than secular institutions in providing educational or professional employment opportunities.

All these may be omens, but they are hard to believe. At this moment in the eyes of most militants from Mexican-American communities, the Catholic Church plays only a peripheral role in the solution of social and economic problems of their people.

Because poverty is visible and dramatic, little attention is given those Catholic Mexican-Americans dispersed in nondepressed neighborhoods throughout most communities. Needs for these groups require thoughtful action in parishes yet unaccustomed to the presence of an ethnic minority.

Caught in the conflict, too, are moderate Mexican-Americans who are committed to improving the condition for the many disadvantaged Chicanos and at the same time look to the Church for religious leadership. A painful ambivalence is evident in their deliberations over the present situation. Whatever their personal dilemma, few visualize major improvements to the multiple needs of Mexican-Americans without a prolonged period of searching confrontation.

Failing in the reformation of the present leadership, the Catholic Church will continue to diminish in essential religious and personal importance for many Mexican-Americans. Whether they may turn in greater numbers to other denominations for spiritual and religious needs or simply drop out and assume a nonreligious posture becomes speculative.

The great hope is the new order of priests and nuns. They may succeed in keeping alive a flame of faith and hope. If this fails, the meaning of the Catholic Church in America will surely continue an inevitable decline in the life of the Mexican-American community.

chapter 9

# Cultural Identity

Mexican-American studies have led to whimsical assumptions regarding the mother culture. The goal today is to achieve coherence from the coming together of the Iberian culture of the conquistadores,[1] the middle cultures of the Mexicans,[2] the American-Indians of the Southwest, and of course, the input of the Puritan ethic. An acceptable rationale is yet to be attained, but this may come with time.

It must be said at this point that

. . . the study of Mexican national character remains in the hands of philosophers and essayists, who, however . . . with few exceptions [have been] impressionistic, intuitive, or speculative. . . .[3]

A sense of integrity then dictates the conclusion that

. . . the modal Mexican personality, based on the ideas of the foregoing writers . . . [is] quite inconclusive, and that a great deal of scientific fieldwork is required.[4]

Today, social scientists, Anglo-Americans, and militant Chicanos use folklore with abandon to explain Mexican-Americans. This source is used to give substance to strained conclusions. These approaches tend to be simplistic and the worse for disregarding the best available in sociological and anthropological data. For example, whatever the original need for the

1. Henry B. Parkes, *A History of Mexico* (Boston: Houghton Mifflin Co., 1950); William H. Prescott, *The Conquest of Mexico*, 2 vols. (New York: E. P. Dutton [n.d.]).
2. Helen Augur, *Zapotec* (Doubleday-Dolphin, 1954); Sylvanus G. Morley and George W. Brainard, *The Ancient Maya*, 3rd ed. (Stanford, Calif.: Stanford University Press, 1956); George Vaillant, *Aztecs of Mexico* (Garden City, N.Y.: Doubleday, Doran and Co., Inc., 1944); Victor W. Von Hagen, *World of the Maya* (New York: The New American Library, Inc., Mentor Books, 1960).
3. Gordon W. Hewes, "Mexicans in Search of the 'Mexican,' Notes on Mexican National Character Studies," *American Journal of Economics and Sociology* 13, no. 2 (January 1954):210.
4. Ibid., p. 223.

construct of *machismo* and fatalism in the many writings, today these seem poor pretenses for an analysis and explanation of the Mexican-Americans of the 1970s.

The result of these exercises then become the bases for many of the current efforts to explain Mexican-Americans. It can be argued, of course, that the culture of Mexico is inextricably tied to the fusion of the Spanish interloper and the indigenous people of Mexico. The *mestizo* of Mexico today is a biologic and cultural product of the two. Others to be sure, the Moor for example, all have become a part of this, but by now it must be a totally different amalgam. It is this *mestizaje* with other factors added which needs explanation if the Mexican-American is to be understood.

Adding confusion and fogging expectation for a plausible interpretation about the roots of Mexican-Americans is the esoteric dabbling of the dilettantes based on the essays of two well-publicized Mexican essayists, Paz and Ramos.[5] Their published ventures—literary efforts to discover the roots of the Mexican character and steeped in Adlerian and Surrealistic theory— are questionable bases, however, for understanding Chicanos. The hasty and uncritical embrace of the interpretations of these essayists by Mexican-Americans or Anglos can only limit the exploration of many alternatives and can serve to restrict progress in legitimate areas of scholarly study.

America with its abundance in literate resources can hardly grasp the reliance on the word-of-mouth process used in the perpetuation of folk fables. Fact and fancy are passed on from one generation to another. Anglo-Americans cannot appreciate, perhaps, the limited disciplined study of any kind, Anglo or Mexican, used in recording the realities of Mexican culture.

The new faces emerging today in the Southwest of America are the Mexican-Americans. In the chronicles these faces are referred to as Hispanos, Spanish-Americans, Latin-Americans, and Chicanos. For all the attributes of a Mexican culture, for all the dynamism of a Puritan ethic, for all the mysticism of an Indian heritage, these Mexican-Americans must be vastly different people than their ancestors as they are touched, shaped, and tempered by human forces. The basic question "Who and what is the Mexican-American?" has only been touched lightly. The period of careful documentation and exacting study is yet to emerge in full bloom. It is important to note that Mexican-Americans are not new on the American scene, but they are now being perceived differently. This may be the great difference and may give direction to future developments.

Today, many are honestly trying to understand Mexican-Americans and to use these insights in improving the worlds of work, play, learning, and

5. Octavio Paz, *The Labyrinth of Solitude: Life and Thought in Mexico* (New York: Grove Press, Inc., 1962); Samuel Ramos, *Profile of Man and Culture in Mexico* (New York: McGraw-Hill Book Co., 1963).

shelter. Mistakes have been committed. Some were unfortunate; others were products of ignorance, insensitivity, or exploitation. In any case, many Chicanos believe they have been and are exploited, and they generate hot emotions over this thought.

Writers agree on some generalizations about Mexican-Americans. They share in culture universals. For example, strands of the Spanish language run throughout the total experience. The Spanish names of cities, streets, parks, buildings, rivers, creeks, historical events, and personalities are constant reminders.

Secondly, the *mestizaje* of the Mexican-American is pronounced. It is visible. The mixture of European and Indian has given birth to *La Raza*. Even people bypassed in the Southwest because of geographic isolation slowly but surely succumb to the culture of *mestizaje*.

The third universal that weaves itself in and out of today's Mexican-American is religion. The image of the *conquistadores* arriving in the New World with flag, sword, and cross has left an imprint on lives and cultures. The Mexican without a Catholic faith would indeed be someone other than who he is. Over the centuries the Church, though changing a bit in outward form under the influence of the Indian culture, provided a pillar of strength for a people who were subdued politically, economically, socially, and at times spiritually. And while the *indio* and the *mestizo* found solace in the spiritual strength of the Church, the Church itself as an institution oppressed and exploited and severely limited the potentiality of the Mexican. This historic fact today explains, in part, the severe ambivalence of some Mexican-Americans toward the Catholic Church. This animosity surely explains the attraction of Protestantism in some cases, though the majority of the Mexican-Americans today—seventy to ninety percent—continue Catholic in faith.

Cultural awareness workshops, seminars, and classes are receiving merited attention. These are especially overdue in education, public health, and other social services. But awareness is a total societal need and is not exclusively a sole concern of these occupational groups. It applies to all segments of communities. While agreement is reached on the need for in-service and preservice experiences, inquiries must be raised over the nature of the experience and content matter. Only honest and unafraid questions will lead to fruitful long-term outcomes.

Stereotypes to be liquidated are the siesta-prone, sarape-cloaked, sombrero-covered, guarache-clad, tortilla-chewing, and tequila-drinking Mexican. His favorite pose in the contemporary art bulletin board and in commercial advertising is reclining against a cactus in the midafternoon. Stereotypes like these should be ruthlessly attacked for what they are—pernicious views about an ethnic group.

Americans of Mexican descent are not going to vanish, so these stereotypes cannot simply be eliminated without something else in their place. It is
about these substitutions or realistic replacements that questions must be
raised. These questions should be raised by all concerned—Anglo-Americans
as well as Mexican-Americans—who have a stake in a democratic society.

Reviews of many commercial as well as professional publications show
a consistent pattern of ethnic characteristics attributed to Mexican-Americans. These tend to be rural folk societal traits. Whatever the original
validity of these in Mexico or in the old Southwest, legitimate questions are
in order today about using a rhetoric of this type as an explanation. How can
it accurately or justly describe an estimated five to six million chiefly urban
Americans of Mexican descent today?

Many of the attempts to nurture sensitivity and awareness of Mexican-
Americans treat the issue as if Mexican-Americans were a simple-minded
monolith differing from each other only in the length of their mustaches or
their singing or playing the guitar. This type of indiscriminate projection
reaches the ridiculous. Naive acceptance of these cartoons contributes little
or nothing to the elimination of alienation and social conflict in any group.

The available literature tends to picture Mexican-Americans in a negative fashion. The treatment is consistent in its rural stereotypes or in its total
omission from the text. Mexican-Americans, in other words, are excluded
from historical or literary roles.

The Mexican-American family is typically described as unique, and
each of its family members has a distinct role. It is patriarchal and father is
the breadwinner. Mother is a self-effacing personality preserving home and
family. The good wife is subservient to her husband, and her goal in life is
pleasing him and seeing that the children receive affection and attention.

But contrary to this in many homes in the Southwest today mother
works and she has a decisive voice, if not the chief one, in family decisions,
management of finances, and care of the children. Wives often supplement
family income with outside employment—just as the Anglo-American wives
do. Children are individualistic and are just as spoiled and as saucy with their
parents as their Anglo-American counterparts. Certainly many restrictions
of the activities for boys and girls in the family are not greater for Chicanos
than for average Anglo-American youth.

Where geographic or social isolation is a fact, old-country culture ways
may be observed, but then this may be more a case of poverty or low-income
syndromes, and these apply to all hard-core poor.

A clearer understanding of Mexican-American families must admit
the potential range of total possibilities in family organizations found in
Mexico as in the United States. They will surely be mixtures of all types possible, and patterns may be unclear. Only this may be valid.

Mexican families are described as large because children are loved, they are assets, and family planning is not typical. Statistically, Mexican-American families tend to be larger than the average American family, but it must be noted this relationship is found high between socioeconomic rather than nationality classes. Poor people throughout the United States tend toward larger families than they can support economically. Children are no longer the economic assets they once were. An industrialized and techno-logical society restricts until a late age the entry of the young into the world of work. Inspections of vertically mobile middle-class Mexican-Americans reveal family-size patterns not unlike those of middle-class Anglos. To be sure, children are loved and they are protected, but this hardly seems much different than most families anywhere.

The extended family is without a doubt one of the warmest traits attrib-uted to Mexican-Americans. What greater sense of unity and security can there be than to know that grandparents, aunts and uncles, cousins, nephews and nieces, and different godparents can be counted on for support in times of grief and need as well as enjoyed in times of abundance and gaiety? Yet partly because of the increased ease of physical mobility of families, fewer *barrios* or segregated neighborhoods exist in the old sense in many urban areas. Old customs and family traditions and behavior patterns, already weak a generation ago, are dying out totally. The extended family, so cherished in concept by romanticists, if observed at all in today's families, must be but a shadow of what it was in its historic heyday.

The lazy-man image, the *mañana* complex of Chicanos, is explained as present-time orientation. This construct is so well entrenched in narra-tives that even Mexican-Americans remind each other of appointments say-ing, "We mean American time, not Mexican time!" Then these same persons scurry away responding to the same duress of mechanistic time that moves their Anglo friends. Insurance agents, as an example, can attest to the fact that future planning is indeed an important element in the lives of today's Mexican-Americans.

Whatever the Mexican-American may be in America today, he *can* be better understood by a study of his cultural and historical background. But considerable restraint must be exercised to prevent incorrect interpretations based on popular and even demagogic stances. Competent and committed inquiry will continue to be a primary requisite before valid conclusions may be drawn.

# chapter 10

# Mexican-Americans Today

A few studies have been selected from the current literature to illustrate recent trends. Obviously, more material is available, but a comprehensive listing is not possible.[1] The departure from popular views and the inconclusiveness of some of the data suggest the need for continued investigations on matters Mexican-American.

Ernesto Galarza, who has spent much of his lifetime in civil combat in behalf of the Spanish-speaking of America, contributes reflective and insightful views into the nature of the basic problem which Mexican-Americans, especially, face today.[2] Are Mexican-Americans strangely unique as a subgroup in America? Mexican-Americans indeed suffer from many ills, but it must not be overlooked that they are one of the many ethnic minority groups in America. *The status of Mexican-Americans is understood by what happens to the groups they belong to:* trade union, Roman Catholic, hardcore poor, political minority power, and the like. In addition to this, America as a whole is obsessed—not Mexican-Americans alone—by its facelessness, its loneliness, and its alienation; many others in America are also excluded. Within the ethnic group gross variations in sharing the goods and services of America are evident. Though it may cool the ardor of speechmakers, essentially, Mexican-Americans who comprise two and one-half percent of the total population of the United States cannot in a numerical sense be considered a "sleeping giant." The dilemma confronting Mexican-Americans is that the key decisions are made within the majority group structure which is where the power lies.

How persistent are culture traits and behavior? Popular accounts suggest only minor change, but a recent study in Utah found that many resident

---

1. Doctoral dissertations about Mexican-Americans completed the last ten years are listed on pages 90–95.
2. Ernesto Galarza, "Minorities: Mirror of Society" (Paper presented California Council for the Social Studies Annual Conference, 1969).

Mexican-Americans as well as those in migrant labor no longer observe many of the Mexican culture traditional rituals.[3] They are no longer important. Contrary to popular literature, Mexican-Americans eligible to vote make use of the right. It is believed that low occupational status and limited educational achievement, rather than social discrimination, are the chief problems facing many Mexican-Americans.

The notion of *machismo*, or the cult of masculinity, is one of the excitatory planks in the rhetoric of the culture reversionists. This cult may exist among some Mexicans, but it is also found in all other world groups; further, it appears to be more a phenomenon of lower socioeconomic classes than of ethnic differences. A study of a Mexican mestizo village in the center of Mexico demolishes long-time beliefs of the romanticists.[4] Findings were not a total repudiation of all that is written about Mexican folkways, but *machismo* begs a new definition. Women are generally portrayed in the literature as submissive and subordinate to men. This may be a gratifying sentiment to males, but the study indicates the truth to be otherwise. Conflict between husband and wife is the expected rather than the atypical relationship. Where the wife strays in adulterous behavior, tradition calls for the betrayed male to leave or to kill the woman. This does not happen. Rather, Mexican women are independent and *muy macha*, and it is the men who return to the hearth. The conclusion is reached that *machismo* is "a pseudo-role . . . a ghost, a vestige that lingers in songs, and movies, the decayed remnants of a code. . . ."[5]

Current stereotypes picture Chicanos all crowded in cultural *barrios*. How true is this? It should be said first that most *barrios* are ethnically mixed, so any vision of a solidly-packed community of Mexican-Americans is usually misleading.

The findings of a California study in the city of Pomona found Mexican-Americans quite free of the *barrio*. Over one-third of the group studied lived completely outside the *barrio* in neighborhoods of their choice.[6] Most Mexican-Americans classified in the semiskilled, skilled, and white-collar occupational groups were found to be upwardly mobile, but this did not mean that they tended to reject their ethnic identity. Another interesting contradiction relates to religion. Contrary to common opinion, Catholics were found to be more upwardly mobile than Protestants, and interestingly, those indi-

3. Helen M. Crampton, "Acculturation of the Mexican-American in Salt Lake County Utah (Ph.D. dissertation, University of Utah, 1967).
4. Lola R. M. Schwartz, "Morality, Conflict and Violence in a Mexican Mestizo Village" (Ph.D. dissertation, Indiana University, 1962).
5. Ibid.
6. Fernando Penalosa, "Class Consciousness and Social Mobility in a Mexican-American Community" (Ph.D. dissertation, University of Southern California, 1963).

viduals who stated no religious affiliation tended to be downwardly mobile.

Social class differences had little relationship to the use of Spanish-language communications media. But it was apparent here that facility with the English language was closely associated with occupational improvement. *The losing of lower-class culture rather than ethnicity is most related to mobility upward.* Accurate and acceptable descriptions or definitions must be created for the many kinds of Mexican-Americans emerging. In short, the diversity within the Mexican-American, and by extension to all Spanish-speaking groups in America, must be recognized.

What of cultural alienation which is reported so frequently in Mexican-American youth? School programs for Mexican-Americans must consider culture factors. First, the culture similarity or the variants within the Mexican-American students must be determined. A simplistic view, perhaps too frequently expressed today, suggests that all Mexican-descent students are culturally alike. This is not the case. A recent doctoral study finds that high school Spanish-Americans (or Mexican-Americans) are very much acculturated and that they respond to the same value orientations as do Anglo-American students.[7] Observations suggest that these students suffer no culture conflict in going to school.

In addition, it was found that Anglo-American teachers responded sensitively to differences between Mexican-Americans and Anglo-Americans. These findings, while not disproving all, clearly contradict much that is written today about culture conflict of Mexican-Americans on the one hand and the insensitivity of teachers on the other.

Spanish-Americans, at least those in school, may be expected to fall on a continuum of acculturation from very Mexican to very Anglo-American. It seems highly valid to consider socioeconomic factors as the chief problems; certainly the indiscriminate application of polar Mexican value orientations to all these students impedes educational and social planning.

The learning of English in America is a basic requisite, though not sufficient in itself, for participating fully in the scheme of things. Recently schools have begun to use the "Teaching of English as a Second Language" approach in helping young Mexican-Americans learn the English language. How helpful is TESL? Though potentially helpful, *it is no panacea.* This approach has not lived up to expectations and has deteriorated soon into perfunctory drill.[8] In educating Mexican-American children, those basic skills and learnings

7. Fred E. Romero, "A Study of Anglo and Spanish-American Culture Value Concepts and Their Significance in Secondary Education" (Ed.D. dissertation, University of Denver, 1966).
8. Eva R. Borrego, "Teaching English as a Foreign Language to Children: First Three Grades" (Ph.D. dissertation, The Catholic University of America, 1968).

necessary for mobility and self-determination are objectives to be achieved. The mother tongue, Spanish, is used in the initial stages with children who speak the language at home, but as soon as possible, Spanish and English change positions in use and English becomes the primary language and Spanish the secondary one. Hopefully, schools will enable a choice and the students will elect to continue the study of Spanish so that they in fact become bilingual, fluent in both English and Spanish. Conclusions in this study are straightforward: Mastery of English is basic for optimal opportunities in America, but Spanish is still needed to give security, identity, and a sense of pride.

Are all Mexican-Americans alike? Findings in a recent study indicate clearly that much of the rhetoric about "Mexican-American" culture orientation and behavior needs to be sifted with care to separate truth from myth. Results of this study refute common stereotypes. In an introductory note the report states that

. . . those studies and reports currently available about the Spanish-speaking of America, or Mexican-Americans, tend to emphasize the "culture of poverty" aspects of the socioeconomically poor of the Mexican-American group. Emphases continue to be on traditional and stereotyped views of simple societal folkways and their anachronisms in an age of lunar orbiting. In other words, the literature and the common lecture about Mexican-Americans are about the poor, the disadvantaged, and the quaint.[9]

A random sample of thirty-one Mexican-Americans was selected. The procedure consisted of tape-recorded oral interviews and a written questionnaire completed by each respondent.

Findings show that Mexican-Americans of the sample who graduate from colleges and universities do not conform to any one stereotype. In varying degrees they are individualistic, articulate, ambitious, civic- and political-minded; they belong to organizations, are urbanized, and feel well prepared for their occupations.

College graduates continue to relate emotionally and actively to ethnic concerns and groups; yet they are also involved in community activities and professional organizations. There is an expressed attachment for the Spanish language and the Mexican culture, but at the same time there is an identity with the Anglo-American culture and the English language.

Family ties and friends within the ethnic group continue to be strong; yet many respondents have close personal ties with Anglo-Americans.

Marriages seem to be stable—intermarriages, though occurring, were not part of the study—and most are Catholic and attend church with some

9. Y. Arturo Cabrera, "Profiles of Mexican-Americans Who Graduate from College" (Faculty Research Project, San Jose State College Foundation, June 1969).

regularity. They tend to read books, magazines, and newspapers at least as frequently as the general population.

Mexican-Americans who graduate from colleges and universities are highly mobile and acculturated, and while they reflect histories of obstacles and some social ambivalence in their lives, they are optimistic, they believe in themselves, and they expect to continue to progress in their chosen professions.

Parental support for continued education for this group while not always financial was strong; so it seems the popular comment that "Mexican-American parents don't care about education" needs revision.

This study found that educated Mexican-Americans do not perceive or do not agree on the nationally known or prominent Mexican-American personalities. Does this mean no Mexican-Americans reach positions of status and prestige? Does it reflect a blackout by news and literate media? This is an example, perhaps, of omission of the group's role in historical and contemporary events.

If the key to self-determination is entry into and completion of higher education programs, how well do Chicanos fare? Generally, the total Spanish-surname enrollment in four-year colleges and universities throughout the nation continues at a low ebb.[10] Recent efforts through federally funded education opportunity programs are expected to make an impact, but comprehensive reports are not yet available on the unequivocal effectiveness of these programs. A study of Spanish-surname enrollment at one college illustrates what may be a general status in higher education.

The 1963–1964 Mexican-American enrollment at this college was 2.2 percent of total enrollment.[11] The Spanish-surname population of the state is ten percent, so the data suggest a gross underenrollment of Mexican-Americans at the college. This figure is consistent with average enrollments throughout the Southwest.

A number of interesting observations may be made about the findings. Conceding an underenrollment of Mexican-Americans, the difference between Mexican-American women and Anglo women numbers enrolled is not large. This finding challenges the general belief that Mexican-American girls are not encouraged and do not attend colleges and universities in any numbers because of familial and culture restraints.

10. A selected showing of 1968 enrollment data in the Southwest suffices to illustrate the underenrollment. The University of New Mexico clearly exceeds the efforts of other institutions. Mexican-American enrollment was as follows: University of California, Berkeley, 496 (1.9 percent); University of Texas, Austin, 838 (3.4 percent); University of Arizona, Tucson, 1,116 (4.9 percent); University of Colorado, 249 (1.3 percent); and University of New Mexico, Albuquerque, 1,711 (11.7 percent).
11. Y. Arturo Cabrera, "A Survey of Spanish-surname Enrolled Students, San Jose State College, 1963–1964" (A study at San Jose State College, 1964).

When these findings are compared to the 1966–1967 follow-up study, the increase in enrollment for Mexican-Americans exceeded total college growth by 27 percent.[12] This was attributed to a search-and-find program conducted by the Mexican-American Community Services Agency and the college LEAP Program (Latent Educational Abilities Project)[13] in operation that academic year. Other findings show that 85 percent of the Mexican-American students reside permanently within a sixty-mile radius of the college. Attrition from college for Mexican-Americans was no worse than that of the student population at large throughout the sequence of four college years of study.

Two conclusions follow these data: (1) Living at home is one way Mexican-Americans combat the economics of attending college; and (2) The data do not show an unusual attrition to the group. The major challenge, if this holds true on a wider scale, is getting larger numbers of Mexican-Americans into college.

With a growing activism, the AMAE (Association of Mexican-American Educators, Inc.) concerns itself with educational and social needs.[14] This professional association is increasingly impatient with the lethargy of the system in moving toward effective programs for the solution of educational problems of Mexican-Americans.[15]

These selected examples of recent findings will hopefully stir reflection. Observations and conclusions derived from carefully planned investigations markedly deviate from commonly held stereotypes. Does this mean that all past views are in error? No, this suggests that some firmly held beliefs may be greatly in error or inconclusive because of design or sampling inadequacies. It means a serious commitment for study must generate if data about Mexican-Americans are to be helpful.

Much has been written about the poor and alienated, but the study of the total group with its noted diversity needs undertaking. Until these inquiries are implemented, tightly designed and competently controlled, the bases for judgment and planning will continue shallow. This dedication for open-minded research is the challenge awaiting Mexican-Americans and Anglos alike.

12. Cabrera, "Spanish-surname Students at San Jose State College: A Comparison of 1963–64 and 1966–67" (A study at San Jose State College, 1967).
13. These programs predated subsequent educational opportunities programs for ethnic minority students.
14. Resolutions from the Fourth Annual Convention illustrate this new militancy and are shown in Appendix C.
15. See *American Teacher*, November, 1968, for an account of the East Los Angeles' Chicano protest; *Carta Editorial*, October 31, 1968 (P.O. Box 54624, Terminal Annex, Los Angeles, California 90054).

# chapter 11

# Four Points to the Compass

The available data understandably concentrate on the glaring, unmet, socioeconomic needs of Mexican-Americans as a subgroup. Findings and recommendations about the poor have general acceptance, and this will continue until constructive results make them unnecessary. A need continues for the free exploration of the many possible directions for action, not the least of which are the imaginative projections for the mobilization of the middle-class Mexican-Americans. For example, "How can Mexican-Americans become effective factors in the decision-making processes in the total society rather than exclusively in terms of the hard-core *barrio*?" Underlying this notion is the question, "Where will the effective power for status change come?" And also, only an unhampered approach will give birth to a coherent body of thought expressive of the "Mexican-American ethos" that can serve as a springboard toward identity. These have not occurred, but even worse, current spokesmen shy away from them as viable strategies.

Too many individuals today look for a rationale which supports personal views or by which all the blame can be attributed to others. Needed is a thorough knowledge of past events leading to present conflicts and a willingness to work effectively toward eliminating problems which show many old sores.

The dynamism of the United States is breathtaking. No immigrant group hoping to share in the life of America can escape undergoing marked changes under the impact of the acculturative forces in daily operation. If this is true, what then explains the reported isolation of Mexican-Americans? Will they eventually travel the road as many others have in the past and integrate fully into America? Present in-depth knowledge of the acculturative processes in America is dismally incomplete, but the following views are regarded as reasonable.

Reports of the poverty-prone are filled with the woes of Mexican-Americans and their children. In the early periods of colonization, everyone suffered deprivations in the Southwest, but following the acquisiton of these lands by the United States, the Anglo prospered while the socioeconomic condition of the Spanish-speaking people suffered. These people are part of the generational cycles of poverty in America, of course. All the events leading to this statement are history and require no argument here. For most Anglos, the Hispanic people of America project a "social problems" image today. But what has happened, and this is indicated by recent studies, is that mobility and successes have occurred, though the extent of these await fuller description. This growth has received so little attention, however, that it is lost to *both* Anglos and Mexican-Americans. Little doubt can be entertained today that Mexican-Americans—the Spanish-speaking—are now also in a middle-class category.

Why then is the Mexican-descent group chronically among the ranks of the hard-core deprived? Some reasons are already suggested in this book and in other sources countless of times. But what *cannot* be ascertained with assurance is the explanation attached to the fact that *Mexicans* have been and continue to be the last, great, exploitable supply of unskilled and malleable labor. As Mexicans and their families are imported by America's big-business bosses, these immigrants fill the vacancies created by Mexican-Americans who have moved up and out. Thus, this constant supply of Mexicans feeding in at the bottom of the economic pyramid is guaranteed through the controlled influx of unacculturated, nonindustrialized, and non-urbanized people. To the outsider, no visible change is apparent in the *barrios*, the public schools serving these *colonias*, or in the fields, though in fact mobility takes place in plain sight of everyone. But it is not seen.

What might happen if this source of labor were blocked can only be speculative. Mobility patterns might operate as they have for other past immigrants. However, other questions must be raised. Successive waves of immigrants have come to America, and new immigrants displace the group which arrived earlier. Mobility takes place for the older group, and the new one undertakes learning the new culture and, though not consciously, awaits the eventual arrival of a later and different wave of trusting refugees. And the cycle repeats itself in time. But what if *Mexicans* now represent the *last* wave of immigration for crude labor purposes? Will they too move up the socioeconomic ladder? Will the pool of exploitable Mexicans disappear? Or must *some group* always be at the bottom rung of the pecking order?

The crystal ball becomes hazy at this point, and one can only guess about future events. Encouragingly, Mexican-Americans are moving upward today, and the more society lives its ideology—clear opportunities for men and women commensurate with their abilities and the will to use them —upward movement may then be expected of Mexican-Americans. This conclusion omits, of course, an elaboration of many other complex social forces in play today.

One conclusion which stems from the argument above is that *Mexican-Americans are not going to disappear.* The visibility of Mexican-Americans sharpened by the cultural regeneration and replenishment of the reservoir by the tide from Mexico will continue. And for some Anglos the "social problems" will not have changed. And while the system will continue to reward some Mexican-descent individuals or subgroups, other Chicanos will continue to exhibit the so-called "language and culture" differences which spell trouble to so many social agencies and institutions. Stated another way: An imperative will continue for America to respect, to understand, to plan, and to implement strategies for the release of the human potential in these people for their good as well as the good of American society.

A fascination may be expected to develop and to continue over some of the popularized views of Mexican culture partly because it is a first exposure, not only for Anglo-Americans, but for some Mexican-Americans as well. Notwithstanding the lack of any validation for the assumptions and even though disciplined inquiry is admittedly limited, this "culture" can be expected to be the basis for emotional rhetoric, and countless Mexican-American studies will dwell on *machismo* or *Jorgenegretismo, indigenismo, caciquismo;* inferiority complex; necrolatry, micromania; the *pelado* cult and its justification of alcoholism, double moral standards, personal honor, and amification. And the list will grow and the polarization will grow. Eventually the reality of America may be expected to orient the extremes of emotionalized energies and talents to the job at hand, "Where do the Mexican-Americans go from here?"

In planning alternative strategies, it must be remembered that the isolation of an ethnic group can serve to reinforce tendencies in a community to think of it as a stereotyped subgroup and not as a collection of people with common characteristics but also with great individual differences. Much of this has already occurred.

The hard-to-reach subgroups of alienated Mexican-American youth are a conscious part of the total concern. One young Mexican-American teacher, analyzing conflicts of far-out gangs of Chicanos, said:

> In this group of "Changos" [a derogatory term] there exists a minority within a minority. Most members of this sub-culture have not experienced success in one form or another, as measured by our middle class standards. They come from broken homes, families which are too large; they are doing very poorly in school and are constantly in trouble with authorities. . . .
>
> I believe that this group mentioned (hard core) has experienced humiliation and oppression to the extreme where *they no longer have any sense of values which*

*relate to the dominant society or to the minority group from which they initially identified with. . . .*[1] [emphasis added]

In reviewing data on referrals to the rehabilitation center for juvenile delinquents, this teacher discovered that the greatest referral rates came from a few center-city schools where Mexican-Americans are an overwhelming majority. One junior high school consistently headed the list with the greatest number.

Direct confrontation as a tactic was successful against the educational establishment in the late 1960s. Sharpened to a keen edge by extremists and adopted by militant Mexican-Americans, it has been a most effective tool for encouraging program innovation and as a device for control of positions and staffings within ethnic studies and educational opportunities programs.

In the past, when community-based organizations of Mexican-Americans, and other minorities, raised their voices about educational and other needs, officialdom failed to take any action. Very little hope may be held for a return to the old procedure *unless* a new confidence is established. This will only come about through observed changes in attitudes and behavior.

Some Chicanos are expending much emotion and energy in efforts to "ban" the use of the hyphen from the written word *Mexican-American*.[2] These individuals are understandably irritated by the fact that a hyphenated American is by social definition a second-class citizen. This "campaign" seems a silly and futile wrangle at the moment. With or without a hyphen, or by any name, identifiable outgroups will face predictable conflicts *until* they acquire power—political, economic, and educational—to get done things which they feel are important. It is just that simple. Until this reality is fully accepted and the group's potential is used optimally, no great changes in group status may be reasonably expected. This places a premium on an awareness of group resources, the operation of the political and economic system, and how to mobilize the group potential, often political, in coalition to pursue objectives.

All resources need to be used in solving problems of humans; one of the overlooked resources currently estranged from the movement are those Mexican-Americans who have met the challenges of the contemporary culture with some success. Contrary to expressed views, it is unlikely that many of these individuals possess hidden stores of wealth or unusual community power which they withhold out of sheer whim. Rather, they are Mexican-Americans with a potential for positive interaction with many diverse

1. A course paper presented at San Jose State College, July, 1969. The confidentiality of the writer and the names of schools cited is respected.
2. The hyphen was retained throughout this book. Orthographically the evolution expected is *Mexican American, Mexican-American,* and then *Mexicanamerican.* More important, the hyphen remained as a symbol of the unfinished job in a society which subscribes to an egalitarian and pluralistic ideology.

groups, but most important, with the majority community where the political, economic, and corporate powers lie.

It has been suggested repeatedly that the greatest power for meaningful change in America is with middle-class America. Programs with the potential for far-reaching consequences need the support or at least acquiescence of this socioeconomic segment. Direct sustained opposition from this middle class precludes the launching of the most important programs. It is just that elementary.

Many Mexican-Americans are committed to action leading to improvement. These people have different views about the direction to be followed. Any one of many choices of full-scale programs could be an effective beginning. Individuals and groups operate at all levels of awareness and levels of effectiveness, and in this, Mexican-Americans are like the rest of America. Of course, there are many big goals and many little goals, but it would seem that all goals should be encompassed in the notion of integration of the Mexican-American into America.

Full integration should be a primary goal. This integration does not concede the surrender of a bilingual and bicultural heritage as the price for belonging. Mexican-Americans are marginal today, and it is likely they will continue to be outsiders in the important matters of America until certain conditions are met.

When Mexican-Americans are fully integrated, the following will happen: Mexican-Americans will be elected and appointed to high offices in local, state, and federal government as well as to boards-of-education and blue-ribbon commissions at all levels. Mexican-Americans will be visible in high corporate and entrepreneur leadership and equity throughout the land. Mexican-Americans will be awarded prestigious recognition as professionals in medicine, law, scholarship, social and physical sciences, fine arts, or in any field of human effort where talent and the spark of genius create their own expression. Mexican-Americans will philosophize or seek tranquillity in communion with their creator and say it at a cultivated and literate level. Mexican-Americans will be counted among the policy- and decision-makers of commerce, industry, fine arts, government, and military. Mexican-Americans will be conspicuously wealthy and will be patrons of fine arts, politics, and philanthropy.

When the dual cultures are accepted and enjoyed freely, when artificial restraints are removed, then Mexican-Americans will fully contribute to and share in the promise of America.

## BIBLIOGRAPHY

ADAMIC, LOUIS. *A Nation of Nations*. New York: Harper and Brothers, 1945.
ANDERSON, ODIN W. *Health Services in a Land of Plenty*. Health Administration Perspectives No. A7, University of Chicago, 1968.

ANGEL, FRANK. "Program Content to Meet the Educational Needs of Mexican-Americans." National Conference on Education Opportunities for Mexican-Americans, Austin, Texas, April 25–26, 1968.

*As the Child Reads . . . : The Treatment of Minorities in Textbooks and Other Teaching Materials.* National NEA-PR&R Conference on Civil and Human Rights in Education, Washington, D.C., February 8–10, 1967.

BAGDIKIAN, BEN H. *In the Midst of Plenty.* New York: The New American Library Inc., Signet Books, 1964.

BANFIELD, EDWARD C. *Big City Politics.* New York: Random House, Inc., 1965.

BILLINGTON, RAY ALLEN. "Bias in History Textbooks." *Saturday Review* 49, January 15, 1966, pp. 59–61, 80–81.

BLATT, GLORIA T. "The Mexican-American in Children's Literature." *Elementary English*, April 19, 1968, pp. 446–451.

BORREGO, EVA R. "Teaching English as a Foreign Language to Children: First Three Grades." Ph.D. dissertation, The Catholic University of America, 1968.

CABRERA, LUIS G. *Plantas Curativas de Mexico: Propiedades Medicinales de las Más Conocidas Plantas de Mexico Su Aplicación Correcta y Eficaz.* Quinta Edicion. Edicion Ciceron, Mexico, D.F., 1958.

CABRERA, Y. ARTURO. "Profiles of Mexican-Americans Who Graduate From College." Faculty Research Project, San Jose State College Foundation, June 1969.

———. "A Study of American and Mexican-American Culture Values and Their Significance to Education." Ed.D. dissertation, University of Colorado, 1963.

———. "A Survey of Spanish-Surname Enrolled Students, San Jose State College, 1963–64." A study, San Jose State College, 1964.

———. "Spanish-surname Students at San Jose State College: A Comparison of 1963–64 and 1966–67." A study, San Jose State College, 1967.

*Californians of Spanish Surname.* State of California Division of Fair Employment Practices, San Francisco, California, May 1964.

CAMPA, A. L. "Mañana Is Today." In *Southwesterners Write,* edited by T. M. Pearce and A. P. Thomason. Albuquerque: University of New Mexico Press, 1946.

CHICANO ETHNIC STUDIES CLASS. "Problems of Retention as Seen by Mexican American Students." Conference, California State College, Long Beach, May 15–17, 1969.

CRAMPTON, HELEN M. "Acculturation of the Mexican-American in Salt Lake County Utah." Ph.D. dissertation, University of Utah, 1967.

"Foundations Snub Mexican-Americans." *San Jose Mercury,* April 2, 1969.

GALARZA, ERNESTO. "Minorities: Mirror of Society." California Council for the Social Studies, 1969, pp. 20–26.

———. In *Southwest Council of La Raza.* First Annual Report, March, 1969.

GAST, DAVID K. "Characteristics and Concepts of Minority Americans in Contemporary Children's Functional Literature." Ed.D. dissertation, Arizona State University, 1965.

GOMEZ, ANNA NIETO, and VASQUEZ, J. ANTHONY. "The Needs of the Chicano on the College Campus." Conference, California State College, Long Beach, May 15–17, 1969.

GUERRA, MANUEL H. "The Retention of Mexican American Students in Higher Education with Special Reference to Bicultural and Bilingual Problems." Conference, California State College, Long Beach, May 15–17, 1969.

HARRINGTON, MICHAEL. *The Other America: Poverty in the U.S.* Baltimore: Penquin Books, Inc., 1962.

*Health Wanted: For Millions of Americans.* . . . A Preliminary Report from the Health Task Force of the Urban Coalition, 1819 H. Street, N.W., Washington, D.C. 20006, July, 1969.

HEWES, GORDON W. "Mexicans in Search of the 'Mexican', Notes on Mexican National Character Studies." *American Journal of Economics and Sociology* 13, 2 (January 1954).

KRANYIK, ROBERT D. "A Comparison of the Images of Mexico Portrayed in Elementary Social Studies Textbooks and Possessed by Connecticut and Mexican Teachers." Ph.D. dissertation, University of Connecticut, 1965.

KRUG, MARK M. "History Textbooks in England and in the United States." *Elementary English,* December 1963, pp. 821–824.

MEREDITH, ROBERT ADDISON. "The Treatment of United States-Mexican Relations in Secondary United States History Textbooks Published Since 1956." Ed.D. dissertation, New York University, 1968.

MEYER, D. SWING. *The Winning Candidate.* New York: James H. Heineman, Inc., 1966.

MONTEZ, PHILIP. "Mexicanismo vs. Retention." Conference, California State College, Long Beach, May 15–17, 1969.

PENALOSA, FERNANDO. "Class Consciousness and Social Mobility in a Mexican-American Community." Ph.D. dissertation, University of Southern California, 1963.

PEREZ, MONTE E.; DIAZ, MARIA; and MARTINEZ, OSCAR. "Retention of Mexican American Students in College." Conference, California State College, Long Beach, May 15–17, 1969.

*Proceedings of the Conference on Increasing Opportunities for Mexican American Students in Higher Education.* California State College, Long Beach, May 15–17, 1969.

*Proceedings of the National Conference on Educational Opportunities for Mexican Americans.* Austin, Texas, April 25–26, 1968.

ROBINSON, DONALD W., ed. *As Others See Us: International Views of American History.* Boston: Houghton Mifflin Co., 1969.

ROMERO, FRED E. "A Study of Anglo and Spanish-American Culture Value Concepts and Their Significance in Secondary Education." Ed.D. dissertation, University of Denver, 1966.

SAMORA, JULIAN. In "Mexican-American Seminar." Mimeographed. Phoenix, Arizona, January 18, 1963.

SANCHEZ, GEORGE I. In "Mexican-American Seminar." Mimeographed. Phoenix, Arizona, January 18, 1963.

SAVETH, EDWARD N. *American Historians and European Immigration: 1875–1925.* New York: Columbia University Press, 1948.

SCHWARTZ, LOLA R. M. "Morality, Conflict and Violence in a Mexican Mestizo Village." Ph.D. dissertation, Indiana University, 1962.

*Seasonal Farm Worker Report.* San Jose City Health Department, California, 1964.

SLOTKIN, AARON N. "The Treatment of Minorities in Textbooks." *Strengthening Education.* New York City Board of Education 16 (1964). In *Education Digest,* October 1964, pp. 21–23.

SMITH, MARGUERITE. "English As a Second Language for Mexican Americans." National Conference on Educational Opportunities for Mexican-Americans, Austin, Texas, April 25–26, 1968.

SMITH, MILDRED MULKIN. "An Analysis of Basal Reader Stories with Cultural Settings Outside the United States." Ed.D. dissertation, Indiana University, 1959.

*Teaching About Other Countries and People in Elementary School.* Department of Elementary School Principals, National Education Association, June, 1960.

ULIBARRI, HORACIO. "Educational Needs of the Mexican-American." National Conference on Educational Opportunities for Mexican-Americans, Austin, Texas. April 25–26, 1968.

UNESCO. *Bilateral Consultations for the Improvement of History Textbooks.* July 1953. Nendln, Liechtenstein: Kraus Reprint, Ltd., 1966.

UNITED MEXICAN AMERICAN STUDENTS. "Retention of the Chicano Student As a Comprehensive Program Unit of the Mexican Student Organization." Conference, California State College, Long Beach, May 15–17, 1969.

WATSON, JAMES B., and SAMORA, JULIAN. "Subordinate Leadership in a Bicultural Community." *American Sociological Review* 19, August 1954, pp. 413–421.

WILSON, HERBERT B. "Evaluation of the Influence of Educational Programs on Mexican-Americans." Conference, California State College, Long Beach, May 15–17, 1969.

WOLFE, MANSELL WAYNE. "The Images of the United States in the Hispanic American Press: A Content Analysis of News and Opinions of This Country Appearing in Daily Newspapers from Nineteen American Republics." Ph.D. dissertation, Indiana University, 1963.

WOODS, SISTER FRANCES JEROME. *Mexican Ethnic Leadership in San Antonio, Texas.* Washington, D.C.: The Catholic University of America Press, 1949.

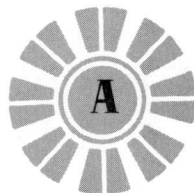

# Resolutions: Third Annual Mexican-American Issues Conference
### Sacramento City College, Sacramento, California
### April 19-21, 1969

*Economic workshop*

That the membership of this body herewith commit itself to the full support of any and all activities essential to the development of a strong Mexican-American economic base.

*Educational workshop*

*Motivation (recruitment)* That State and local MAPA Education Committees pressure legislators (Federal, State and local) to fund and expand EOP programs and Upward Bound programs.

That state and local MAPA Education Committees work in two teams to pressure for legislation to bring into the colleges more Chicano students; to change the quota system and to pressure for using the 4 percent rule exclusively for Third World Students; one team working on funding, the other on recruitment procedures (abolition of quotas, etc.).

That MAPA work diligently for *any* program related to Chicanos, disseminate information on the various programs, endorse and support said programs.

*Chicano studies* That MAPA go on record as a strong supporter of Chicano studies and Third World College.

That MAPA actively pressure the State Legislative [sic] to make funding available for these studies and colleges.

That MAPA actively participate in formulation and help to implement such programs where they now do not exist.

*Resolved* statements only are shown. Permission through the courtesy of Mr. Abe Tapia, State President, Mexican-American Political Association, 2415 Whittier Blvd., Los Angeles, California 90023.

*Role of Chicano administrators and faculty* That MAPA have a regular meeting and/or conference in the community with Chicano faculty and administrators.

That MAPA have a communication set up with Chicano faculty and administrators for purposes of dissemination of information and for assistance.

That MAPA support Chicano administrators and faculty in their encounters with the Establishment.

That EOP funds be made permanently available to Chicano students in the colleges and universities of California and controlled and administered by the local minority community.

That (a) both interdepartmental majors and Standard Designating Subjects credentialing be extended to include both Studies and Credentials on peoples of Latin-American descent as well as Afro-American descent; (b) that this program not be restricted to a given date in the future, but extended indefinitely.

That the bills passed in the legislature or being considered student oppression, [sic] be eliminated.

That (Senate Bill 28, English as a Second Language) be refunded and expanded.

That MAPA support the Job Corps concept and urge that these centers not be curtailed.

That Headstart funds be permanently granted and expanded as needed by the communities.

That MAPA oppose discriminatory and harsh practices leading to harassment by schools and urge that local school authorities revoke them.

*Farm labor workshop*

To notify all organized labor of the resolutions adopted at this Mexican-American conference that deal with the betterment of the farm worker.

That a committee be formed to work with the United Farm Workers Organizing Committee, AFL-CIO to achieve NLRA coverage.

That state MAPA organize International Safeway Day on May 10th and henceforth continue participation in the Safeway campaign.

That this conference support Bill AB 1202 to include male employees within jurisdiction of the Industrial Welfare Commission for purposes of minimum wage, maximum hours and working conditions.

To redefine "minor" to mean any person under 18, rather than 21, years of age and authorize establishment of lower minimum wage for minors based on differences in productivity, but in no case less than 75 percent of the adult minimum wage.

That this Mexican-American conference demand unemployment insurance for all farm workers in the state and nation.

## *Housing workshop*

That this conference of Spanish-speaking Organizations insist that the Departments of Housing and Urban Development and local housing authorities and redevelopment agencies hire Spanish-speaking Information Officers to contact our communities to inform them of the nature, extent and availability of housing programs for the Spanish-speaking.

That this conference demand that the Department of Housing and Urban Development cease and desist from further perpetuation of the conspiracy against our people and immediately recruit and hire as many Mexican-Americans as would accurately reflect their population in the Southwest.

That demand of our State Legislature a change of laws to allow local communities, especially farming communities, so local counties can build homeless, family-less, singlemen farm workers' living quarters and farm labor centers.

## *Manpower workshop*

That this conference go on record and support Mexican-American key administrators in the Department of Labor and who recently have been removed by the Department of Labor from a decision-making position to a staff position; and

That not only these Mexican-Americans be placed in decision-making positions but that other Mexican-Americans be added to the Department of Labor.

## *Political action workshop*

That the Mexican-American community will no longer tolerate tokenism or denial or the exercise of self-determination; and

That it will no longer be redisposed to support any particular political party, but will support the party which makes its candidates and issues relevant to the Chicano needs.

That the Chicano will research each community and pertinent issues affecting our community in order to assess these problem areas and work effectively toward their solution;

That the Chicano will seek and support capable and responsible Chicano candidates to further strengthen our own effective political organization for political action to realize the full potential of our community.

That all resolutions adopted by this conference be designated as MAPA policy and implemented as such.

That the national president and his officers be delegated the responsibility to carry this mandate.

That each local MAPA chapter exercise with discretion the political autonomy delegated to assess each situation and initiate measures to develop wherever necessary political alliances and coalitions.

*Welfare workshop*

That each county provide free day-care centers to low income families in which the family head is engaged in employment, training for employment, or attending school.

That welfare rights organizations be encouraged by the county, and the county provide a private attorney to deal with the legal complexities, and the harassment members as a result of their activities.

That current educational standards be revised so welfare departments and welfare recipients can most benefit from human resources available in the community.

That welfare agencies create two new job classifications: (1) Social Service Worker Spanish-speaking-bicultural and (2) Eligibility Worker Spanish-speaking-bicultural. That the knowledge of the Spanish language and culture be equivalent to 60 units of the present educational requirements in both of these job classifications.

That Spanish-speaking, bicultural workers be given Spanish-speaking caseloads, and/or complete charge of services and eligibility of Spanish-speaking clients.

That welfare agencies actively recruit candidates for these two job classifications until the percentage of Spanish-speaking, bicultural workers equals the percentage of Spanish-speaking clients.

*Legislative issues workshop*

That a preplanning conference be held prior to the next legislative issues conference consisting of MAPA, all sponsoring organizations, local Chicano groups and young people organizations and leaders, and that the MAPA state leadership take full responsibility for this preplanning conference.

That future Mexican-American legislative conferences also include a work-shop on economic development.

# Resolutions: West Coast Coalition of Priests and Sisters Working with the Spanish-Speaking
### 2020 East San Antonio Street
### San Jose, California 95116

I. *Organization*
   A. That local organization of priests and/or sisters working with Spanish-speaking people be formed.
   B. That coalitions of these groups be formed on a regional, national and international level.
   C. That the role of these organizations will be supportive of the Chicano and the 3rd World Movements.
   D. That special emphasis be given to support the Chicano Youth Movement.
   E. That a full-time co-ordinate be hired for the West Coast Coalition.

II. *Deaconate Program*
   A. That there be an immediate start of a lay and clerical deaconate program within the Spanish-speaking community.
   B. We demand the revision of the qualifications set down by the USCC so as to encourage the participation of indigenous Spanish-speaking leaders in the Deaconate program.

III. *Seminarians*
   A. That seminaries, both major and minor, establish ethnic studies programs of the Spanish-speaking people.
   B. That those seminarians interested in working with Spanish-speaking communities be given special, positive training programs, that show creativity and adaptability.

By permission of West Coast Coalition of Priests and Sisters, January 12, 1970.

    C. That these special training programs for seminarians, because of the desperate situation of the Spanish-speaking people, be given top priority financing.

    D. That the special training and ethnic studies spoken of in the above resolutions be applicable to novices, sisters, priests and lay deacons.

IV. *Former Priests*

    A. That those priests who have left the active ministry and are interested in working with the Spanish-speaking be invited and encouraged to work with the needs of the Spanish-speaking people.

    B. That those priests in individual cases be restored to the active ministry.

V.     That teams of priests and sisters be recruited and freed to work without limitations of parish boundaries with Spanish-speaking people in each area.

VI.     That each area have people involved in laying out a pastoral plan for Spanish-speaking people showing its priorities and their implementation.

VII. A. That resources of the diocese be distributed without regard to ability to contribute.

    B. A projects review board with laymen of both majority and minority groups, in addition to priests, determine the manner of Church expenditures in diocese with representation.

    C. That there be a full disclosure of parish and diocesan finances.

    D. That preference be given to self-help programs for the poor with the money going directly to them rather than through Church or other agencies.

    E. That special attention be given to job training, low-cost housing, and scholarships for the poor.

    F. That personnel and spiritual resources of the diocese be distributed equally among all members of the diocese.

VIII.     We recommend the establishment of Chicano-oriented Episcopal Vicars for the Spanish-speaking on the West Coast.

IX. A. That the priests work toward directing the people on learning their political rights and powers.

B. That in conjunction with other Chicano groups we take steps to establish a lobby at state, county, and local level.

C. We support the right of priests to take direct action on specific issues.

D. The West Coast Coalition take stands on public issues.

    1. This power be focused on issues selected on the basis of their importance for the whole Spanish-speaking community, rather than on issues affecting only a small group.

X.    That programs be developed to make the Anglo community aware of the pressing needs of the Spanish-speaking and to challenge people of good will to support the Spanish-speaking cause.

XI.    We support the organizing efforts of the UFWOC.

XII. A.    That a committee formed by this Coalition in conjunction with local groups present the resolutions of this conference to their Bishops.

B.    That if these resolutions are not sufficiently recognized by the Bishop that the Coalition take appropriate action.

XIII.    That this Coalition make its existence and aims known to the Bishops, Senates, Associations, and to community groups of Chicanos on the West Coast.

XIV.    Effective enforcement of Affirmative Action Clauses of Federally funded programs and adequate legislation to benefit the Farm Workers.

XV.    That we support Catolicos Por La Raza in Los Angeles and the priests involved with them and that we express this support to the priests, to Father Urban, to Cardinal McIntyre, to the *Tidings*, to Catolicos Por La Raza and to the press.

XVI.    That some mechanism for draft counseling be set up for Chicanos.

XVII.    That local groups of priests consider moving out of their rectories to live more closely with the Spanish-speaking people.

# Resolutions: Fourth Annual Convention
## Association of Mexican-American Educators, Inc.
### San Diego, California
### March 14-16, 1969

1. That the Federal government increase the funding of Title VII, ESEA, to $150,000,000 for the year 1970 to provide a minimum of $100 per child for relevant educational opportunities for the Mexican-American.

2. That in spite of complaints already registered to the Frito-Lay, Incorporated, they have continued the commercial and Frito-Lay, Incorporated, should be condemned for such practice. AMAE should call a boycott of all products by Frito-Lay, Incorporated.

   Secondly, that Packard Bell has also contributed to the negative image of Mexican-Americans. AMAE should call a boycott of all products produced by Packard Bell and they should be condemned.

   Thirdly, that AMAE commend the Equal Employment Commission for the vote taken in Los Angeles yesterday to file a "Pattern Suit" against the television and movie industries for their discriminatory practices against Mexican-Americans. We also urge that the U.S. Attorney General proceed with this suit.

3. That Mexican-American children who are educationally hampered by the adjustment problems of bi-culturalism and bi-lingualism regardless of the parents' income be allowed to take full part in all government projects under Titles I and VII.

4. That the Department of Education Bureau of Bi-lingual Education initiate several operational models.

5. That the Office of Education solicit school districts and institutions of higher learning for institutes directed at developing curriculum for Mexican-American children.

*Resolved* statements only are shown.

6. That AMAE support Constitutional change which would establish the voting age at 18; thus including large numbers of responsible citizens in the decision-making process.

7. That AMAE support the concept of the Mexican-American Educators Study [data on educational commitment throughout the Southwest] and urge that appropriate funding be made so as to assure a high level of sophistication and quality in the conduct of this study.

8. That AMAE support the establishment of a joint committee of the State Assembly and Senate to investigate, develop, and establish an adequate program of bi-lingual education for the children, and adults of this state; and be it further resolved

   That the membership of this Association stand ready to provide the help necessary to assure a comprehensive program of bi-lingual education.

9. That the State Department of Education, Bureau of Inter-Group Relations be instructed to utilize Spanish surname and teacher identification as the means for identifying youngsters of Spanish ancestry rather than the more convenient term "Spanish surname."

10. That AMAE lend the entire impact of its organizational influence to the Bill [Bagley re integration effort] and strongly endorse its passage by contacting legislators in Sacramento encouraging them to vote favorably on this bill.

11. That AMAE pledge full support to continuing and expanding ESEA, Migratory Program, Teacher Corps, Bi-lingual Education Act, the Economic Opportunity Act, and other federal projects which have brought new hope and opportunity to Mexican-American youth.

12. That AMAE spur support and cooperate with "maestros para mañana," a cooperatively developed program by NEA and affiliates and the AMAE.

13. That AMAE pursue a vigorous campaign aimed at State Legislators so that they will provide the necessary funds for ESL [English as a Second Language] programs in California and throughout the Southwest.

14. That AMAE (1) support the actions of the Chicano student movement of pursuing better education, (2) pledge funds to help defray bail and fines imposed on incarcerated students involved in these movements, (3) encourage educator support of student movements in their individual chapters, (4) protect financially, publicly, and morally educators arrested, beaten, or ostracized as a result of their support of Chicano

students, and (5) denounce the use of unreasonable police force in educational institutions.

15. That a more aggressive and determined campaign to establish chapters throughout the five Southwestern states be initiated immediately.

16. That a leadership training conference be convened as soon as possible for the purpose of focusing and coordinating the efforts of the various AMAE chapters in their respective states.

17. That the AMAE work to the establishment of a Mexican-American Education unit or component of NEA [National Education Association].

18. That the AMAE president communicate with the main offices of Sears and Montgomery Ward and demand that this oversight [omission of models in their advertising] be corrected so that Mexican Americans will be part of the models shown in these mail order catalogs and thereby a better cross-section of the people of our country will be shown.

19. That AMAE oppose AB 126, Bee. We hold the opinion that it is too early to establish any state-wide standards for the employment of In-structional Aides other than those standards which refer to health and public safety.

20. That AMAE negotiate with federal, state, and municipal governments, labor and private industry to devise a plan or plans for remuneration to needy families with children participating in summer and post-secondary education programs.

> (s) Robert R. Flores, Chairman of the Resolutions Committee.

# glossary

| SPANISH | ENGLISH |
|---|---|
| arroz | rice |
| barrio | ghetto, neighborhood |
| bolillo | Anglo, a derogatory term |
| caciquismo | bossism |
| caída de la mollera | fallen fontanel |
| la causa | the cause, movement |
| chango | Mexican-American youth, monkey |
| chicano | Mexican-American, an old term revived with varied acceptance |
| compadre | godparentage relationship |
| conquistador | Spanish conqueror reference |
| curandero | faith healer |
| empacho | indigestion |
| es tiempo | it is time |
| frijoles | beans |
| indigenismo | indigenous roots, in a glorified sense |
| indio | Indian |
| Jorgenegretismo | hypermasculinity, from film actor Jorge Negrete |
| machismo | cult of masculinity |
| maíz | corn |
| mal (de) ojo | evil eye |

| | |
|---|---|
| mal puesto | sorcery |
| malinchismo | betrayal of one's people, from Cortez' Indian mistress Malinche, sellout |
| mañana | tomorrow |
| mestizo | Biologic mix of Spanish and Indian |
| peón | laborer, low social class person |
| pelado | a nobody, downtrodden |
| La Raza | sense of peoplehood |
| señorita | Miss, young lady |

# general bibliography

ACUNA, RUDOLPH. *Story of the Mexican Americans: The Men and the Land.* Junior High School text. New York: American Book Company, 1970.

ALLEN, STEVE. *The Ground Is Our Table.* Garden City, N.Y.: Doubleday and Co., Inc., 1966.

AUGUR, HELEN. *Zapotec.* Garden City, N.Y.: Doubleday-Dolphin, 1954.

BANCROFT, HUBERT HOWE. *History of Mexico.* New York: The Bancroft Co., 1914.

BARKER, GEORGE C. *Pachuco, an American-Spanish Argot and Its Social Functions in Tucson, Arizona.* Tucson: University of Arizona Press, 1958.

BARRIO, RAYMOND. *The Plum Plum Pickers.* Novel. Sunnyvale, Calif.: Ventura Press, 1969.

BEALS, RALPH. "Culture Patterns of Mexican-American Life." *Proceedings of the Fifth Annual Conference, Southwest Council on the Education of Spanish-speaking People,* pp. 5–13. Los Angeles: Pepperdine College, January 12–20, 1951.

BOATRIGHT, MADY BOGGIN, ed. *Mexican Border Ballads and Other Lore.* Austin, Tex.: Folk-Lore Society, 1962.

BOGARDUS, EMORY S. *The Mexican in the United States.* Los Angeles: University of Southern California Press, 1934.

BRAND, DONALD D. *Mexico: Land of Sunshine and Shadow.* Princeton, N.J.: D. Van Nostrand Co., Inc., 1966.

BRUSA, BETTY WAR. *The Bracero.* New York: Pageant Press, Inc., 1966.

BRUSSELL, CHARLES B. *Disadvantaged Mexican American Children and Early Educational Experiences.* Austin, Tex.: Southwest Educational Development Corporation, 1968.

BURMA, JOHN H. *Spanish-Speaking Groups in the United States.* Durham, N.C.: Duke University Press, 1954.

BUSTAMANTE, CHARLES J., and BUSTAMANTE, PATRICIA L. *The Mexican-American and the United States.* Intermediate School-level text. Mountain View, Calif.: Patty-Lar Publications Ltd.

CAMPA, ARTHUR L. *Spanish Folk-Poetry in New Mexico.* Albuquerque: University of New Mexico Press, 1946.

CHRISTIAN, JANE, and CHRISTIAN, CHESTER, JR. "Spanish Language and Culture in the Southwest." In *Language Loyalty in the United States: The Maintenance and Perpetuation of Non-English Mother Tongue by American Ethnic and Religious Groups*, edited by Joshua A. Fishman, pp. 280–317. New York: Humanities Press, Inc., 1966.

CLARK, MARGARET. *Health in the Mexican-American Culture: A Community Study*. Berkeley: University of California Press, 1959.

COOKE, W. Henry. *Peoples of the Southwest*. Freedom Pamphlet. Chicago: Anti-Defamation League of B'nai B'rith, 1951.

CRAWFORD, FRED R. *The Forgotten Egg*. A Study of the Mental Health Problems of Mexican-American Residents of the Good Samaritan Center, San Antonio, Texas, © 1961.

CUMBERLAND, CHARLES C. "The United States-Mexican Border: A Selective Guide to the Literature of the Region." *Rural Sociology* (Supplement) 25:2, June 1960.

CURRENT, TOM, and MARTINEZ, MARK INFANTE. . . . *and Migrant Problems Demand Attention*. State of Oregon Bureau of Labor, Salem, Oregon, September 1959.

DEL CASTILLO, BERNAL DIAZ. *The Discovery and Conquest of Mexico*. Translated by A. P. Maudslay. New York: Harper. 1928.

DOBIE, J. FRANK. *Coronado's Children*. New York: Literary Guild of America, 1931.

———. *A Vaquero of the Brush Country*. Dallas: The Southwest Press, 1929.

DWORKIN, ANTHONY GARY. "No Siesta Mañana: The Mexican-American in Los Angeles." Chapt. 8 in *Our Children's Burden*, edited by Raymond W. Mack, pp. 387–439. New York: Random House, Inc., Vintage Books, 1968.

EELLS, K., and others. *Intelligence and Cultural Differences*. Chicago: University of Chicago Press, 1951.

ESPINOSA, JOSE MANUEL. *Spanish Folk-Tales From New Mexico*. New York: Published by the American Folk-Lore Society, G. E. Stechert and Co., New York Agents, 1937.

FAIR EMPLOYMENT PRACTICES COMMISSION. *Californians of Spanish Surname: Population, Education, Employment, Income*. 455 Golden Gate Avenue, San Francisco, Calif., May 1964.

FAULK, ODIE B. *Land of Many Frontiers: A History of the American Southwest*. New York: Oxford University Press, 1968.

FORBES, JACK D. *Mexican-Americans, A Handbook for Educators*. Berkeley, Calif.: Far West Laboratory for Educational Research and Development, 1967.

GALARZA, ERNESTO. *Merchants of Labor: The Mexican Bracero Story*. San Jose, Calif.: The Rosicrucian Press, Ltd., 1964; Santa Barbara, Calif.: McNally and Loftin, Publishers.

———. *Spiders in the House and Workers in the Field*. Notre Dame, Ind.: University of Notre Dame Press, 1970.

———; GALLEGOS, HERMAN; and SAMORA, JULIAN. *Mexican-Americans of the Southwest*. Santa Barbara: McNally and Loftin, Publishers, 1970.

GAMIO, MANUEL. *Mexican Immigration to the United States: A Study of Human Migration and Adjustment.* Chicago: University of Chicago Press, 1930.

GARNER, CLAUD. *Wet Back.* New York: Howard McCann, 1947.

GRIFFITH, BEATRICE W. *American Me.* Boston: Houghton Mifflin Co., 1948.

GUERRA, MANUEL, and CABRERA, Y. ARTURO. *An Evaluation and Critique of 'The Mexican American Studies Project' A Ford Foundation Grant Extended to the University of California At Los Angeles.* Mexican American Political Association (Calif.), 1966.

HASELDEN, KYLE. *Death of a Myth.* New York: Friendship Press, 1964.

HEFFERNAN, HELEN, ed. *Teachers Guide to the Education of Spanish-Speaking Children.* California State Department of Education Bulletin, vol. 16, no. 14, 1952.

HELLER, CELIA S. *Mexican-American Youth: Forgotten Youth at the Crossroads.* New York: Random House, Inc., 1966.

HENDERSON, RONALD W. *Environmental Stimulation and Intellectual Development of Mexican-American Children—An Exploratory Project.* Tucson: University of Arizona, 1966.

HERNANDEZ, LUIS F. *A Forgotten American: A Resource Unit for Teachers On the Mexican American.* Anti-Defamation League of B'nai B'rith, 1969.

KELLEY, ISABEL. *Folk Practices in North Mexico: Birth Customs, Folk Medicine, and Spiritualism in the Laguna Zone.* Austin: University of Texas Press, 1965.

KIBBE, PAULINE R. *Latin Americans in Texas.* Albuquerque: University of New Mexico Press, 1946.

LANDES, RUTH. *Latin Americans of the Southwest.* Americans All Series. New York: Webster Division, McGraw-Hill Book Co., 1965.

LEA, AURORA LUCERO-WHITE. *Literary Folklore of the Hispanic Southwest.* San Antonio, Tex.: The Naylor Co., 1953.

LEWIS, OSCAR. *Five Families: Mexican Case Studies in the Culture of Poverty.* New York: Basic Books, Inc., Publishers, 1959.

———. *Pedro Martinez: A Mexican Peasant and His Family.* New York: Random House, Inc., 1964.

MCWILLIAMS, CAREY. *North From Mexico: The Spanish-Speaking People of the United States.* New York: J. B. Lippincott Co., 1943.

MADSEN, WILLIAM. *The Mexican-Americans of South Texas.* New York: Holt, Rinehart and Winston, Inc., 1964.

MANUEL, HERSCHEL T. *Spanish-Speaking Children of the Southwest: Their Education and the Public Welfare.* Austin: University of Texas Press, 1965.

MARTINEZ, RAFAEL. *My House Is Your House.* New York: Friendship Press, January 10, 1964.

MEAD, MARGARET, ed. "The Spanish Americans of New Mexico." In *Cultural Patterns and Technical Change*, pp. 151–177. New York: The New American Library, Inc., Mentor Books, 1955.

*The Mexican-American.* Paper prepared for the U.S. Commission on Civil Rights, 1968.

*The Mexican-American, a New Focus on Opportunity.* Testimony presented at the Cabinet Committee hearings on Mexican-American Affairs, El Paso, Texas, October 26–28, 1967. Washington, D.C.: U.S. Government Printing Office, 1968.

*Mexican-American Study Project.* Graduate School of Business Administration, University of California, Los Angeles. Reports: 1965–1968.
"Education and Income of Mexican-Americans in the Southwest."
"Mexican Immigration to the United States: The Record and Its Implications."
"Revised Bibliography."
"Residential Segregation of Minorities in the Urban Southwest."
"The Burden of Poverty."
"Intermarriage of Mexican-Americans."
"The Schooling Gap: Signs of Progress."
"Mexican-Americans in a Midwest Metropolis: A Study of East Chicago."
"The Mexican-American Community."
"The Spanish-Americans in New Mexico."
"Mexican-Americans in Southwest Labor Markets."

MORIN, RAUL. *Among the Valiant.* Los Angeles: Borden Publishing Co., 1963.

MORLEY, SYLVANUS G., and BRAINARD, GEORGE W. *The Ancient Maya.* 3rd ed. Stanford, Calif.: Stanford University Press, 1956.

NAVA, JULIAN. *Mexican Americans Past, Present and Future.* Junior High text. New York: American Book Co., 1968.

NELSON, EUGENE. *Huelga: The First Hundred Days of the Great Delano Grape Strike.* Delano, Calif.: Farm Worker Press, 1966.

NICHOLSON, IRENE. *The X in Mexico: Growth Within Tradition.* Garden City, N.Y.: Doubleday and Co., Inc., 1966.

PARKES, HENRY B. *A History of Mexico.* Boston: Houghton Mifflin Co., 1950.

PAZ, OCTAVIO. *The Labyrinth of Solitude: Life and Thought in Mexico.* (Spanish ed., 1950) New York: Grove Press, 1961.

PINCHON, EDGCOMB. *Viva Villa.* New York: Harcourt, Brace and Co., 1933.

———. *Zapata, the Unconquerable.* New York: Doubleday Doran, 1941.

PITT, LEONARD. *The Decline of the Californios: A Social History of the Spanish-Speaking Californians, 1846–1890.* Los Angeles: University of California Press, 1966.

PRESCOTT, WILLIAM H. *The Conquest of Mexico.* 2 vols. New York: E. P. Dutton and Co., Inc., Everyman's Library.

RAMOS, SAMUEL. *Profile of Man and Culture in Mexico.* New York: McGraw-Hill, 1951.

ROBERTS, MARTA. *Tumbleweeds.* Novel. New York: G. P. Putnam's Sons, 1940.

ROBINSON, CECIL. *With the Ears of Strangers: The Mexican in American Literature.* Tucson: University of Arizona Press, 1963.

ROMANO, OCTAVIO I., ed. *El Espejo: The Mirror.* Berkeley, Calif.: Quinto Sol Publications, Inc. n.d.

RUBEL, ARTHUR J. *Across the Tracks: Mexican-Americans in a Texas City.* Austin: Published for the Hogg Foundation for Mental Health by the University of Texas Press, 1966.

RUIZ, RAMON EDUARDO. *The Mexican War.* New York: Holt, Rinehart and Winston, Inc., 1963.

SAMORA, JULIAN, ed. *La Raza: Forgotten Americans.* Notre Dame, Ind.: University of Notre Dame Press, 1966.

SANCHEZ, GEORGE I. *Concerning Segregation of Spanish-Speaking Children in the Public Schools.* Inter-American Education Occasional Papers IX, University of Texas, December, 1951.

————. *Forgotten People: A Study of New Mexicans.* Albuquerque: The University of New Mexico Press, 1940.

SAUNDERS, LYLE. *Cultural Differences and Medical Care: The Case of the Spanish-Speaking People of the Southwest.* New York: Russell Sage Foundation, 1954.

Smith, Justin H. *The War With Mexico.* Vol. 2. New York: The Macmillan Co., 1919.

STEINER, STAN. *La Raza: The Mexican Americans.* New York: Harper and Row, Publishers, 1970.

TAYLOR, PAUL S. *An American-Mexican Frontier, Nueces, Texas.* Chapel Hill, N.C.: University of North Carolina Press, 1934.

————. *Mexican Labor in the United States.* Migration Statistics IV. Berkeley, California: University of California Publications in Economics, vol. 12, no. 3, 1934.

TIREMAN, L. S. *Teaching Spanish-Speaking Children.* Rev. ed. Albuquerque: University of New Mexico Press, 1951.

*El Tratado de Guadalupe Hidalgo, 1848: Treaty of Hidalgo, 1848.* Sacramento: Telefact Foundation in Cooperation with California State Department of Education, 1968.

TUCK, RUTH D. *Not With the Fist: Mexican-Americans in a Southwest City.* New York: Harcourt, Brace and Co., 1946.

ULIBARRI, HORACIO. *Social and Attitudinal Characteristics of Migrant Ex-Migrant Workers—New Mexico, Colorado, Arizona, and Texas.* University of New Mexico, College of Education, 1965.

VAILLANT, GEORGE. *Aztecs of Mexico.* Garden City, N.Y.: Doubleday, Doran and Co., Inc., 1944.

VILLAREAL, JOSE ANTONIO. *Pocho.* Garden City, N.Y.: Doubleday and Co., Inc., 1959.

VON HAGEN, VICTOR W. *World of the Maya.* New York: The New American Library Inc., Mentor Books, 1960.

WRIGHT, DALE. *They Harvest Despair: The Migrant Farm Worker.* Boston: Boston Press, 1965.

ZEA, LEOPOLDO. *The Latin-American Mind.* Translated by James H. Abbott and Lowell Dunham. Norman: University of Oklahoma Press, 1963.

# doctoral dissertations

ADKINS, PATRICIA GUYNES. "An Investigation of the Essentiality of Idioms and Figures of Speech in the Education of Bilingual Students in the Ninth Grade in Texas and New Mexico." University of Colorado, 1966. (67–10,023)

AMEJTIAN, ARMISTRE. "The Effects of a Pre-school Program Upon the Intellectual Development and Social Competency of Lower-class Children." Stanford University, 1966. (66–6316)

BAKER, EDWIN DENNIS. "A Study of the Administrative Provisions Providing for the Needs of Non-English Speaking School-age Children in Grades Kindergarten Through Sixth in Selected Schools in the Area of Greater Washington, D.C." The Catholic University of America, 1968. (69–8889)

BERNARD, JUDITH ANN. "Mexico as Theme, Image, and Contribution to Mythology in the Poetry of Octavio Paz." University of Wisconsin, 1964. (64–3911)

BODINE, JOHN JAMES. "Attitudes and Institutions of Taos, New Mexico." Tulane University, 1967. (67–17,901)

BOLGER, PHILIP ALBERT. "The Effect of Teacher Spanish Language Fluency Upon Student Achievement in a Bilingual Science Program." St. John's University, 1967.

BORREGO, EVA R. "Teaching English as a Foreign Language to Children: First Three Grades." The Catholic University of America, 1968. (69–9127)

BOWEN, JEAN DONALD. "The Spanish of San Antonio, New Mexico." University of Texas, 1960.

BOYD, LOLA ELIZABETH. "The Image of Emiliano Zapata in the Art and Literature of the Mexican Revolution." Columbia University, 1965.

BRACK, GENE MARTIN. "Imperious Neighbor: The Mexican View of the United States 1821–1846." University of Texas, 1967. (67–14,805)

BRANSFORD, LOUIS ALEXANDER. "A Comparative Investigation of Verbal and Performance Intelligence Measures at Different Age Levels with Bilingual

The *Dissertation Abstracts* was the basic source for the search on doctoral studies about Mexican-Americans. Studies from institutions not affiliated with the micro-filming service are irregularly shown. Only studies later than 1960 are listed in the effort to make new information known, and wherever possible, the order number is indicated. Further information is available from University Micro-films A Xerox Company, 300 North Zeeb Road, Ann Arbor, Michigan 48106.

Spanish-speaking Children in Special Classes for the Mentally Retarded." Colorado State College, 1966 (67–1098)

BRENNAN, J. E. "A Study of the Channels of Communication Used by Spanish-named Residents of San Antonio, Texas." Louisiana State University and Agricultural and Mechanical College, 1968. (69–4455)

BRONSON, LUISE F. "Changes in Personality Needs and Values Following Conversion to Protestantism in a Traditionally Roman Catholic Ethnic Group." University of Arizona, 1966. (66–10,219)

BROOKS, MELVIN S. "The Social Problems of Migrant Farm Laborers: Effect of Migrant Farm Labor on the Education of Children. Southern Illinois University, 1960.

BROOKS, RICHARD MARTIN. "The Psychological and Cultural Bases of Magical Disease Beliefs." University of Arizona, 1964. (64–12,814)

Bustrillow, Nena Rola. "Decision-making Styles of Selected Mexican Homemakers." Michigan State University, 1963. (63–6143)

CABRERA, Y. ARTURO. "A Study of American and Mexican-American Culture Values and Their Significance in Education." University of Colorado, 1963. (64–4348)

CASTANEDA, ALBERTA MONDOR. "The Differential Effectiveness of Two First Grade Mathematics Programs for Disadvantaged Mexican-American Children." University of Texas, 1967. (68–4264)

COOKE, EDWIN DAVIS. "Interpersonal Orientation of Elementary Teachers with Mexican-American Pupils." University of California at Los Angeles, 1967. (67–14,297)

COPP, NELSON GAGE. "Wetbacks and Braceros: Mexican Migrant Laborers and American Immigration Policy, 1930–1960." Boston University, 1963. (63–6580)

CRAMPTON, HELEN MICKESEN. "Acculturation of the Mexican-American in Salt Lake County, Utah." University of Utah, 1967. (67–12,352)

DAVIDSON, MARGARET RUTH. "A Comparative Pilot Study of Two First-grade Programs for Culturally Deprived Mexican-American Children." University of Texas, 1967. (67–14,817)

DE HOYOS, ARTURO. "Occupational and Educational Levels of Aspiration of Mexican-American Youth." Michigan State University, 1961. (61–2687)

EARL, CHARLES DOUGLAS. "The Academic Achievement of College Athletes and Non Athletes from Four Ethnic Groups." University of New Mexico, 1968. (69–9242)

GALVAN, ROBERT ROGERS. "Bilingualism as it Relates to Intelligence Test Scores and School Achievement Among Culturally Deprived Spanish-American Children." East Texas State University, 1967. (68–1131)

GAST, DAVID KARL. "Characteristics and Concepts of Minority Americans in Contemporary Children's Functional Literature." Arizona State University, 1965. (66–6902)

GEISS, SALLY ANN. "The Teacher-Student Role Relationship in Junior High Schools Serving Significant Numbers of Disadvantaged Spanish Surnamed Youth." University of Denver, 1967. (68–2396)

GODOY, CHARLES EDWARD. "Variables Differentiating Mexican-American College and High School Graduates." University of Southern California, 1970.

GOERING, JOHN MOYLAN. "Ethnic Consciousness and Political Behavior." Brown University, 1968. (69–9959)

GOLDKIND, VICTOR. "Factors in the Differential Acculturation of Mexicans in a Michigan City." Michigan State University, 1963. (63–6151)

GRASS, ROLAND. "Precursors of the Novel of the Mexican Revolution." Columbia University, 1968. (69–3071)

GRAVES, THEODORE. "Time Perspective and the Deferred Gratification Pattern in a Tri-Ethnic Community." University of Pennsylvania, 1961.

HAMPARES, KATHERINE JAMES. "The Image of the Yankee: The North American Businessman in the Contemporary Novel of Spanish America." Columbia University, 1968. (69–3072)

HARRISON, HELENE WESTBROOKE. "A Methodological Study in Eliciting Linguistic Data From Mexican-American Bilinguals." University of Texas, 1967. (68–4290)

HELLER, CECLIA STOPNICKA. "Ambitions of Mexican-American Youth: Goals and Means of Mobility of High School Seniors." Columbia University, 1964. (64–11,296)

HENDERSON, RONALD WILBUR. "Environmental Stimulation and Intellectual Development of Mexican-American Children: An Exploratory Study." University of Arizona, 1966. (66–15,258)

JACOBSON, LENORE FRANCIS. "Explorations of Variations in Educational Achievement Among Mexican Children Grades One to Six." University of California, 1966 (66–15,306)

JAMESON, GLORIA RUTH. "Development of a Phonemic Analysis for an Oral English Proficiency Test for Spanish-speaking School Beginners." University of Texas, 1967.

JOHNSON, BRUCE E. "Ability, Achievement and Bi-Lingualism: A Comparative Study Involving Spanish-speaking and English-speaking Children at the Sixth Grade Level." University of Maryland, 1962. (63–777)

JOHNSON, HENRY SIOUX. "Ethnic Group Differences in Certain Personal Intellectual, Achievement and Motivational Characteristics." University of Southern California, 1964. (64–13,500)

JONES, LAMAR BABINGTON. "Mexican-American Labor Problems in Texas." University of Texas, 1965. (65–5017)

JOY, KENNETH LEE. "Social Reinforcement as a Function of Children's Linguistic Home Environment." University of South Dakota, 1967. (67–13,222)

KRANYIK, ROBERT DONALD. "A Comparison of the Images of Mexico Portrayed in Elementary Social Studies Textbooks and Possessed by Connecticut," 1965. (66–864)

KRASSOWSKI, WITOLD. "Naturalization and Assimilation Proneness of California Immigrant Populations." University of California at Los Angeles, 1963.

KURTZ, NORMAN RUDOLPH. "Gatekeepers in the Process of Acculturation." University of Colorado, 1966.

LANDOLT, ROBERT GARLAND. "Mexican American Workers in San Antonio." University of Texas, 1965. (66–1936)

LAND, JOHN HART, JR. "Voluntary Associations Among Mexican Americans in San Antonio, Texas: Organizational and Leadership Characteristcs." University of Texas, 1968. (69–6173)

LEMAN, JOHN EDWARD. "Aggression in Mexican-American and Anglo-American Delinquent Males as Revealed in Dreams and Thematic Test Responses." University of Arizona, 1966.

LENTON, MALRY. "The Educational and Occupational Aspirations of Anglo, Spanish, and Negro High School Students." University of New Mexico, 1968. (69–9284)

LIPSHULTZ, ROBERT J. "American Attitudes Toward Mexican Immigration, 1924-1952." University of Chicago, 1962.

LOOS, SALLY ANN. "Cultural Barriers to Communication of Health Information: Special Use of Mexican-American Migrant Workers in California." University of California, 1962.

MACKLIN, BARBARA J. "Structural Stability and Culture Change in a Mexican-American Community." University of Pennsylvania, 1963. (64–3491)

MCCLENDON, JULIETTE JANE. "Spanish-speaking Children of Big Spring—An Educational Challenge." University of Texas, 1964. (65–4330)

MAC MILLAN, ROBERT WILSON. "A Study of the Effect of Socioeconomic Factors in the School Achievement of Spanish-speaking School Beginners." University of Texas, 1966.

MATTHIASSON, CAROLYN WEESNER. "Acculturation of Mexican-Americans in a Midwestern City." Cornell University, 1968. (69–5766)

MEIER, HAROLD C. "The Oral Communication of Health-Disease Beliefs in a Serial Reproduction Experiment." University of Colorado, 1963.

MEREDITH, ROBERT ADDISON. "The Treatment of United States-Mexican Relations in Secondary United States History Textbooks Published Since 1956." New York University, 1968. (69–11,779)

MILLER, ABRAHAM HIRSCH M. "Ethnicity and Political Behavior: An Investigation of Partisanship and Efficacy." University of Michigan, 1968. (69–12,186)

MORPER, JACK. "An Investigation of the Relationship of Certain Predictive Variables and Academic Achievement of Spanish-American and Anglo Pupils in Junior High School." Oklahoma State University, 1966. (67–7264)

NAJAMI, MOHAMED ABDUL K. "Comparison of Greeley's Spanish-American and Anglo-white Elementary School Children's Responses to Instruments Designed to Measure Self-concepts and Some Related Variables." Colorado State College, 1962. (64–5269)

NOSTRAND, RICHARD LEE. "The Hispanic-American Borderland: A Regional, Historical Geography." University of California, Los Angeles, 1968. (69–5340)

NUNEZ, THERON ALDINE JR. "Cultural Discontinuity and Conflict in a Mexican Village." University of California, 1963. (64–5273)

OFFICER, JAMES EOFF. "Sodalities and Systematic Linkage: The Joining Habits of Urban Mexican-Americans." University of Arizona, 1964. (64–9381)

94                                                                    *Doctoral Dissertations*

ORR, RODNEY GERRY. "The Relationship of Social Character and Dogmatism Among Spanish American Young Adults in Three Selected Institutions in New Mexico." University of New Mexico, 1967. (67–11,763)

PAINTER, NATHAN EDWARD. "The Effect of an Instructional Technique in the Modification of Vocabulary Growth of Deprived Bilingual Pupils." Arizona State University, 1965. (65–10,388)

PALOMARES, UVALDO HILL. "A Study of the Role of Mobility in the Acculturation Process of Rural Migrant and Non-migrant Disadvantaged Mexican-Americans in the Coachella Valley." University of Southern California, 1967. (68–5877)

PARSONS, THEODORE WILLIAM JR. "Ethnic Cleavage in a California School." Stanford University, 1966. (66–2602)

PAUCK, FREDERICK GLEN. "An Evaluation of the Self-test as a Predictor of Spanish-speaking First Grade Children." University of Texas, 1968. (69–6200)

PEÑA, ALBAR ANTONIO. "A Comparative Study of Selected Syntactical Structures of the Oral Language Status in Spanish First-grade Spanish-speaking Children." University of Texas, 1967. (68–4327)

PEÑALOSA, FERNANDO. "Class Consciousness and Social Mobility in a Mexican-American Community," University of Southern California, 1963. (64–2598)

PHILLIPS, ROBERT NELSON. "Los Angeles Spanish: A Descriptive Analysis." University of Wisconsin, 1967. (67–10,644)

PLOTT, CURTIS ELLSWORTH. "An Analysis of the Characteristics of Mexican-American and Anglo-American Participants in Co-curricular Activities." University of Southern California, 1967. (67–13,759)

RAMOS, JUAN. "Spanish-speaking Leadership in Two Southwestern Cities: A Descriptive Study." Brandeis University, 1968. (69–8917)

ROGERS, ROBERT B. "Perception of the Power Structure by Social Class in a California Community." University of Southern California, 1962.

ROMANO, OCTAVIO. "Don Pedrito Jaramillo: The Emergence of a Mexican-American Folk-Saint." University of California, 1964. (64–9078)

ROMERO, FRED EMILIO. "A Study of Anglo and Spanish American Culture Value Concepts and Their Significance in Secondary Education." University of Denver, 1966. (66–11,779)

RUBEL, ARTHUR JOSEPH. "Social Life of Urban Mexican-Americans." University of North Carolina, 1962. Published as *Across the Tracks: Mexican-Americans in A Texas City*. Austin: University of Texas Press, 1966.

SATTERFIELD, DONNA MAE. "Acculturation and Marriage Patterns: A Comparative Study of Mexican-American Women." University of Arizona, 1966. (66–15,251)

SCHWARTZ, AUDREY JAMES. "Affectivity Orientations and Academic Achievement of Mexican-American Youth." University of California, Los Angeles, 1967. (68–7483)

SCHWARTZ, LOLA R. M. "Morality, Conflict and Violence in a Mexican Mestizo." Indiana University, 1962. (64–513)

SHASTEEN, AMOS EUGENE. "Value Orientations of Anglo and Spanish American High School Sophomores." University of New Mexico, 1967. (68–3482)

SIMMONS, MARC STEVEN. "Spanish Government in New Mexico at the End of the Colonial Period." University of New Mexico, 1965. (66–4454)

STARK, DONALD STEWART. "Comparative Verb Morphology of Four Spanish Dialects." Cornell University, 1967. (67–16,372)

STARKEY, ROBERTA JOHNSTON. "A Synthesis and Interpretation of Research Findings Which Pertained to Teaching Spanish-speaking Children." Texas Technological College, 1961. (61–6685)

STEEN, MARGARET TROTTER. "The Effects of Immediate and Delayed Reinforcement on the Achievement Behavior of Mexican-American Children of Low-Socio-Economic Status." Stanford University, 1966. (66–8594)

SWADESH, FRANCES LEON. "Hispanic Americans of the Ute Frontier From the Chama Valley to the San Juan Basin 1694–1960." University of Colorado, 1966. (67–10,090)

TAKESIAN, SARKIS ARMEN. "A Comparative Study of the Mexican-American Graduate and Dropout." University of Southern California, 1967. (67–17,705)

TALLEY, KATHRYN S. "The Effects of a Program of Special Language Instruction on the Reading and Intellectual Levels of Bilingual Children." University of New Mexico, 1965. (66–4455)

TSUZAKI, STANLEY MAMORU. "English Influences in the Phonology and Morphology of the Spanish Spoken in the Mexican Colony in Detroit, Michigan." University of Michigan, 1963. (64–898)

ULIBARRI, HORACIO. "Teacher Awareness of Socio-Cultural Differences in Multi-Cultural Classrooms." University of New Mexico, 1960.

VALDES, DANIEL TAPIA. "A Sociological Analysis and Description of the Political Role, Status, and Voting Behavior of Americans with Spanish Names." University of Colorado, 1964. (65–4279)

WEAVER, CHARLES NORRIS. "A Comparative Study of Selective Significant Factors in the Job Performance of the Spanish-surname Employee in Selected Organizations." University of Texas, 1967. (68–4358)

WEAVER, Thomas. "Social Structure, Change, and Conflict in a New Mexican Village." University of California, 1965. (65–8275)

WIEST, GRACE LEONA. "Health Insurance for the Braceros: A Study of Its Development and Implementation Under Public Law 78." Claremont Graduate School and University Center, 1966.

WILSTACK, ILAK MULLER. "Vocational Maturity of Mexican-American Youth." University of Southern California, 1967. (67–13,766)

WOLFE, MANSELL WAYNE. "The Images of the United States in the Hispanic American Press: A Content Analysis of News and Opinions of This Country Appearing in Daily Newspapers from Nineteen American Republics." Indiana University, 1963. (64–5511)

First Spanish Methodist Church, 50
Floating Gardens of Xochimilco, 2
*Frijoles,* 23

Gadsden Purchase, 1
Galarza, Ernesto, 40, 58
Garcia, Alex, 34
Gast, David K., 10
Glossary, 83–84
Gonzales, Robert, 34
Grouping, 15

Harrington, Michael, 25
Hewes, Gordon W., 53
Humphrey, Hubert H., 36

Identity, 8, 17
Image-reflection, 9
Indian, 8
*Indigenismo,* 66
*Indio,* 3, 55
Institutionalized racism, 49
Inter-Agency Committee on Mexican-American Affairs, 10, 39

Jamestown, 1
Jews, 50
*Jorgenegretismo,* 66

Kennedy, Robert J., 36
Kibbe, Pauline R., 5
Kranyik, Robert D., 7
Krug, Mark M., 10

*La Causa,* 36
*La Raza,* 17, 55
Latin-Americans, 7
LEAP (Latent Educational Abilities Project), 63
Leon, Juan Ponce de, 1
LULAC (League of United Latin American Citizens), 33

McCarthy, Eugene, 36
McWilliams, Carey, 5
*Machismo,* 54, 59, 66
Madsen, William, 5, 24
*Maíz,* 23
*Mal ojo,* 24, 25

*Mal puesto,* 24
*Mañana,* 28, 57
Manuel, Herschel T., 12
MAPA (Mexican-American Political Association), 32
MASC (Mexican-American Student Confederation), 42
Materials, literary and instructional, 6
MAYO (Mexican-American Youth Organization), 42
MECHA (Mŏvimiento Estudiantil Chicano de Aztlán), 42
Medical aides, 22
Mental retardation, 24
Mentally retarded, 23
Meredith, Robert Addison, 9
*Mestizaje,* 54, 55
*Mestizo,* 54, 55
Mexican-American Studies, 7, 18, 53
Mexican War 1846–1848, 1, 49
Mexicanism, 4
Mexico, 1
Meyer, D. Swing, 35
Militant(s), 15, 17, 33, 38, 42–53, 67
Minorities, 8, 38, 44, 52
Mitla, 2
Moctezuma, 2
Monte Alban, 2
Montez, Philip, 42
Montoya, Honorable Joseph, 33
Moreley, Sylvanus G., and George W. Brainard, 53
Multicultural, 14, 15

Nahuas, 1
Nava, Julian, 34
"Needs of the Chicano on the College Campus," 47
Negro, 8
New Spain, 48
North American Invasion, 1

Omission, 8
Oñate, Juan de, 1, 39
Ordóñez, Dra. Blanca, 23
Oriental, 8

Parkes, Henry B., 53
PASSO (Political Association of Spanish-speaking Organizations), 33

K